G000252791

MERCEDES-BENZ

MERCEDES-BENZ

TRUCKS TODAY

Eric Gibbins

MOTOR RACING PUBLICATIONS LTD
28 Devonshire Road, Chiswick, London W4 2HD, England

ISBN 0 900549 66 1
First published 1982

Photosetting by Zee Creative Ltd., London SW16
Printed in Great Britain by Netherwood Dalton & Co. Ltd.,
Bradley Mills, Huddersfield, West Yorkshire.

Contents

About the author

ERIC GIBBINS is one of Britain's most experienced and highly respected commercial-vehicle writers with a journalistic career dating from 1953, when he joined *Motor Transport* as an editorial assistant. He subsequently became assistant editor of that journal before taking over the editorship of the magazine *Commercial Vehicles* in 1962. He left journalism for a short period in order to take up a senior public relations appointment within the industry, but by 1970 he was once again writing full-time, soon to become editor and publisher of the *Freight Industry Yearbook* and *Truck & Bus Builder*. His intimate knowledge of all aspects of the commercial-vehicle industry, and in particular of truck design, construction and operation, has been invaluable in ensuring the accuracy and authority of these one-make histories in the TRUCKS TODAY series.

Introduction

Much has been written about Daimler-Benz in the context of the private car, but surprisingly, perhaps, no-one before from outside the company has taken a look at its commercial vehicle development.

This book, therefore, breaks completely new ground to describe the build-up of this West German concern to its present position as the leading European manufacturer of commercial vehicles — and the leading maker in the world of heavy vehicles of over 15 tonnes gross weight.

This has not happened by accident — as I hope readers will realize from the text of this publication, which not only traces product development, but also that of the company in the commercial, manufacturing and development sectors.

In preparing this book, two striking features have emerged. First, the fact that, after the days of Daimler and Benz, there was no personality cult in the company. This is particularly true of the commercial vehicle side of the business. The second is the dynamic progress of the company over the past 20 years — a success which again is attributable not to any individual, but to an extremely strong and far-sighted management.

I must acknowledge particularly the help afforded me in preparing my manuscript by the staff of the Daimler-Benz press office in Stuttgart and the staff of the Archives Department there.

Eric Gibbins

Dr Karl Benz, who was born on November 25, 1844 and died on April 4, 1929.

Born on March 17, 1834, Gottlieb Daimler, who designed the world's first truck, died on March 6, 1900.

Chapter 1

Establishing a reputation

When Gottlieb Daimler and Karl Benz first, and quite independently, produced the first motor cars powered by internal combustion engines they obviously realized that the potential of their inventions was not confined solely to passenger carrying. Whilst giving priority to the development of their private car interests, both created several other types of vehicle.

Daimler and Benz unveiled the first passenger cars in 1886. In the 10 years that followed they announced the first fire-fighting vehicles powered by the internal combustion engine, the first motor bus and, not least, the first motor trucks.

These engineering geniuses recognized right from the start that they were in the business of manufacturing vehicles of all types — not just private cars. It remained part of the Daimler-Benz philosophy when the two names became irrevocably linked in the 1920s and it has remained fundamental to Daimler-Benz thinking ever since. Today, in the 1980s, it can be seen as a main reason for the company's great strength.

It was in September 1896 that Daimler-Motoren-Gesellschaft presented the first Daimler motor truck. It was the first in the world. It was not a one-off, or even a prototype, but one of a range of four models with gross weights of 1,500 kg, 2,500 kg, 3,750 kg and 5,000 kg, powered, respectively, by two-cylinder engines producing 4, 6, 8 and 10 horsepower.

Even at that time, the first sales leaflets produced carried all the basic information essential to encourage the potential buyer to arrive at a decision of whether or not to buy — vehicle weights, engine power output figures, dimensions and prices.

These first vehicles were, of course, rudimentary. They had artillery-type, iron-shod spoked wooden wheels. The driver sat on a wooden bench seat, totally exposed to the weather, steering by a vertical steering column surmounted by a steering wheel in parallel with the vehicle's loading deck. Braking was by a foot pedal linked longitudinally by rods to a transverse rod to which were fitted wooden brake shoes, which applied to the metal rims of the rear wheels when the foot pedal was depressed.

The suspension was, perhaps, the most interesting feature. The rear suspension was by two coil springs, one on each side of the vehicle, mounted directly between the axle beam and a reinforced area below the load platform. At the front, leaf springs were fitted mounted transversely above the axle beam, but bolted to it with the upper leaves inverted and attached to a simple bearing to permit oscillation and steering.

These early designs employed belt drive to the engine. Very soon, however, the engine was repositioned centrally under the vehicle's loading deck. Belt drive was also replaced early on by chain drive, a system which was to continue in use for many years.

Although Karl Benz is considered to have built the first petrol-engined bus — the eight-passenger Landau in 1894 — his first truck appeared in 1898. This, in fact, was a delivery

Built specifically as a truck engine in 1898, this two-cylinder Daimler petrol unit was fitted either at the rear of the vehicle or under the floor.

vehicle and it was sold as such to an American concern for delivery work in New York. It had a payload of 600 kg.

It has to be remembered that the main competitor of the petrol-engined truck at this time was the steam lorry. Internal combustion engines had low power outputs and were generally unreliable. A major step towards greater reliability, however, occurred in 1898 when Daimler installed an engine for the first time with Bosch magneto ignition.

Strangely, perhaps, Daimler found it difficult to sell his motor trucks in Germany. It was in Britain that he found the real market. The first Daimler truck was shown to the public in Britain in 1898 at Sutton Coldfield and then in London. These were the days of field trials and in these competitions the Daimlers met with great success against the main opposition — the steam lorry. The success of Daimler in Britain can be attributed primarily to the efforts of Frederick Simms, who was not only Daimler's commercial agent in England, but the holder of the right to Daimler patents throughout the British Empire.

Several London stores put them into operation and in 1901 Britain's Post Office put its first motor vehicle into operation on a postal service — a Daimler. This sales breakthrough was achieved by G. T. Milnes, who had Frederick Simms as an advisor of Daimler, the vehicles being sold as Milnes-Daimlers.

Dunlop bought a Daimler in 1902 and equipped it with pneumatic tyres; it was not for some years, however, that pneumatics became standard equipment.

Daimler, like Benz, was also active in the USA where, back in 1888, Daimler had signed an agreement with William Steinway, the piano manufacturer, for the latter to build Daimler products, including engines. The American Daimler company built Daimler products in the USA for a number of years.

The USA was also the scene of another world 'first' for it was in Philadelphia in 1902 that the first truck service centre was set up. This provided both maintenance and tow-in services. Daimler's success in the USA, however, was to be short-lived for, although its products found a ready market with stores, bakeries and breweries for delivery duties, a fire at the American Daimler production plant in 1913 put the

Daimler built this, the first purpose-built truck in the world powered by an internal combustion engine, in 1896. It was one of a range of four models with gross weights of 1,500 kg, 2,500 kg, 3,750 kg and 5,000 kg powered respectively by engines producing 4, 6, 8 and 10 bhp.

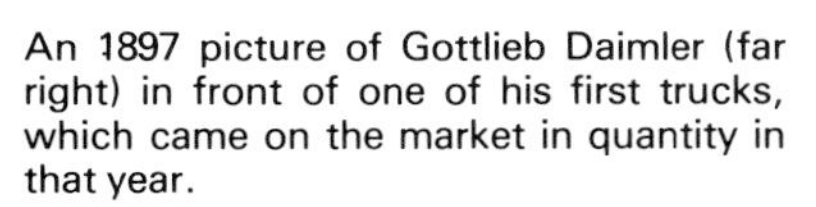
An 1897 picture of Gottlieb Daimler (far right) in front of one of his first trucks, which came on the market in quantity in that year.

Daimler-Motor-Lastwagen.

Im Anschluss an die dem Personenverkehr dienenden Daimler-Wagen werden auch Daimler-Mot
stwagen angefertigt, welche bestimmt sind, den Frachtverkehr zu vermitteln.

Diese Wagen kommen in den nachstehend aufgeführten Grössen zur Ausführung.

Stärke des Motors	HP	4	6	8	10
Zur Beförderung von ca.	Kg.	1500	2500	3750	5000
Gewicht des completen Wagens ca.	Kg.	1500	1900	2500	3000
Preis des completen Wagens	Mark	**5200**	**6400**	**7500**	**8500**
Extra für Heizeinrichtung	Mark	80	80	80	80
Länge des Wagens	ca. m/m.	4500	5600	5700	5700
Breite " "	" "	1500	1700	1800	2000
Höhe " "	" "	1400	1600	1700	1800

This was the first sales leaflet, printed in 1897, for Daimler's first truck range. It had all the essential features for the potential buyer — weights, engine power figures, dimensions and prices.

company out of business at a time when — already — mass production was making itself felt in the American motor industry.

Benz was not far behind Daimler in building trucks. This 1898 Benz built for a payload of 600 kg was sold to the USA for use as a delivery van in New York.

By the end of the nineteenth century, whilst Benz was leading Daimler in terms of annual car output, Daimler was certainly at the front in terms of commercial vehicle development. The success of the company's bus designs in Britain, where they were in widespread use in London (alongside other German makes like Büssing and Benz) was to lead eventually to their acceptance in Germany. This did not occur, however, until 1905, when the Royal Bavarian Postal Authority opened the first German Post Bus service in Upper Bavaria.

Acceptance of vehicles for passenger transport had a significant impact on goods vehicle development and vice versa. Nowhere was this more apparent than in municipalities where motor vehicles for refuse collection and street cleansing were purchased as a result of running buses. Sometimes this happened the other way around and, for example, Glasgow Corporation bought Daimlers for street cleaning in 1902 and later bought buses.

The Daimler company received a major blow in 1900, of course, when on March 6 of that year, Gottlieb Daimler died. His colleague and friend for many years, Wilhelm Maybach, took over from him, however, and under him the company went from strength to strength.

The year before, 1899, had seen the first appearance of the name Mercedes. The name is really associated with private car development, but no book dealing with 'Mercedes' would be complete without mentioning the origin of the name.

Mercedes was the name of the 10-year-old daughter of Emil Jellinek, a rich motoring enthusiast who lived on the French Riviera. He sold Daimler cars there in quite considerable numbers to members of society. He entered a Daimler Phoenix car in the Tour de Nice in 1899 as Herr Mercedes and won first prize. However, the following year, one of the Daimler works drivers, driving an identical Daimler Phoenix,

This was the standard type of Benz truck built in 1900. Note the underfloor engine, vertical steering column, artillery-type wheels and chain drive.

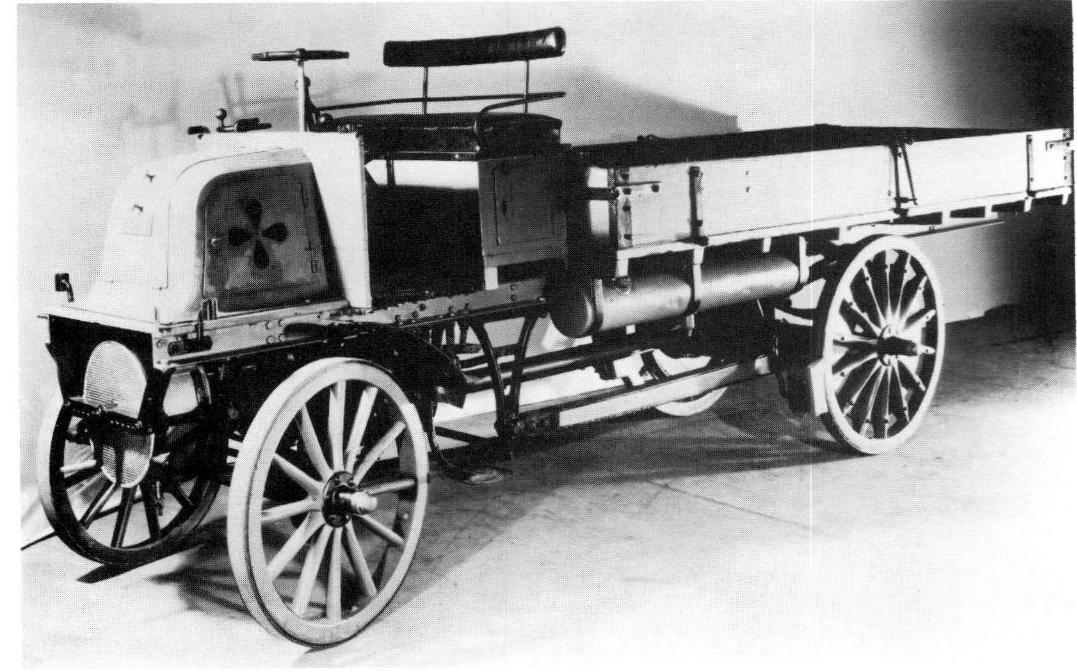

In 1899 Daimler put the engine at the front of the vehicle for the first time. Called the Phoenix, this model was powered by the Daimler 1.53-litre two-cylinder petrol engine producing 5.5 bhp at 600 rpm. It had a payload of 2.2 tonnes.

This 3-tonne payload delivery van fitted with a 6-bhp two-cylinder engine was built by Daimler at its Cannstatt factory in 1900.

was killed in the Nice-La Turbie hill-climb when his car turned over. As a result, Daimler decided no longer to compete in races. Jellinek disagreed. He was convinced that it was too high a centre of gravity and too short a wheelbase on the vehicle that had caused the accident. He asked for a new model with a lower centre of gravity and longer wheelbase and, because he was prepared to place a substantial order for a number of such vehicles, Daimler agreed to build them for him. The order was not placed without strings attached, however. He demanded the sole rights to sell the vehicle in Austria, Hungary, France, Belgium and America under the name Mercedes. The car was a success and the name was registered and patented as a trademark of the Daimler-Motoren-Gesellschaft in 1902.

A lot happened on the truck side of things in the early-1900s. Today, it is often forgotten that the Austro-Hungarian Empire was a major force in European politics and commerce in the years before the First World War. Daimler-Benz's activities in Austria were amongst its most

Daimler bought what is now its Berlin plant at Marienfelde in 1902. Until then it was owned by Motorfahrzeug und Motorenfabrik AG, which built this fleet of electric delivery vehicles for the Berlin firm of Hermann Tietz.

Built by Motorfahrzeug und Motorenfabrik at the Marienfelde factory in 1901, this 5-tonne goods vehicle was the first to be exported to Russia.

Britain was a main customer for Daimler vehicles. This was a brewery vehicle built at the Marienfelde factory in Berlin in 1902.

important, so much so that Paul Daimler, son of Gottlieb, was put in to manage Daimler-Motoren-Gesellschaft in 1902, shortly after that company was formed at Wiener-Neustadt in 1899.

One of the first vehicles it produced under Paul Daimler's leadership was an all-wheel-drive cross-country vehicle which was an immediate success and Austro-Daimler developed an impressive reputation for its innovative engineering.

A popular Austro-Daimler design was a 3-ton 4 × 2 general cargo carrier which had a flat roof and curtain sides. Powered by an Austrian-built, four-cylinder Daimler 12-horsepower engine, it employed shaft drive to the rear axle.

A number of these vehicles went into military service with the Austrian Army, as did the all-wheel-drive models. In fact, the all-wheel-drive principle gave rise to another Austro-Daimler development — a road train powered by one of the most powerful automotive engines up to that time, a six-cylinder unit producing 100 horsepower, built to haul ammunition trains.

Built for carrying bottled beer, this Daimler 3-tonner dates from 1906. It was another product of the Marienfelde plant in Berlin.

An output of 32 bhp was claimed for the four-cylinder engine of this 4-5 tonner built in 1906 at the works of Suddeutsche Automobilfabrik in Gaggenau.

Built at the Unterturkheim factory in 1909, this chain-driven delivery van with 60-bhp engine was one of the first to be fitted with a windscreen.

One of the designers of this vehicle was Ferdinand Porsche, and it was in fact a hybrid as the engine drove a generator with a rated 60-70 kW power output, which in turn drove electric motors hub-mounted in the trailer axles. The innovation did not end there for it was also fitted throughout with air-operated brakes. Later versions of these Austro-Daimler road trains were also built as road-railers with rail and road wheels.

There were parallel developments in Britain where in 1911 the British Daimler concern supplied a road train featuring shaft drive to the centre axle of each three-axled trailer, for use in India.

Apart from its road train development Austro-Daimler went in for producing some very big stuff by the standards of the 1900s, including huge 4 × 4 tractors with six-cylinder 80 and 90-horsepower engines for heavy load-hauling and as heavy artillery tractors.

Everyone in Europe was very aware in the 1900s of the military potential of trucks and the interest for Daimler here centred on the Marienfelde factory in Berlin, which Daimler

The distinctive bonnet, carbide-powered headlamp and radiator of the 8/18-bhp Daimler delivery van built from 1911 to 1913.

A tipper built for Russia at the Marienfelde factory in Berlin. It had a 28-bhp four-cylinder engine and was one of the first vehicles to be built with a propeller-shaft and a rear axle differential.

Built for a payload of 500 to 750 kg, this delivery van was one of a number exported to Russia between 1911 and 1913.

The maximum-capacity outfit of 1912 — a Daimler lorry and drawbar trailer. Note the cab at the front of the trailer to house the driver's mate, who operated the trailer brake.

The first international transport vehicle? This 2-tonne payload Daimler was built for Schenker & Co in 1916 at Marienfelde.

An artillery tractor for the German Army with four-wheel drive built by Krupp-Daimler in 1917. It had a 100-bhp engine and was fitted with ribbed steel 'tyres'.

acquired in 1901. This factory was the headquarters of Motorfahrzeug und Motorenfabrik AG, a company founded in 1897. It was the association of the Berlin company with the London firm of George F. Milnes & Co Ltd which led to the establishment of Milnes-Daimler Ltd in London in 1902. The British company's formation was the direct result of the success of the Marienfelde-built 'Milnes' lorries in the Liverpool truck trials of 1901. Strangely, perhaps, although Daimler was probably the earliest manufacturer to fit propeller-shaft drive in serious quantities, the most popular army lorry types of the 1900 period were chain-driven versions from the Marienfelde factory. They found their way to many parts of the world, not least Russia, whose army ordered some of the first to be built in 1901. These were 4 × 2, 3.4-ton load-carriers operating at 8.4 tons gross and fitted with a two-cylinder 12.9-bhp petrol engine.

At the turn of the century people were still undecided as to which form of power was going to be the winner and there was strong support for electric vehicles and petrol-electrics as well as petrol and steam-powered road vehicles. This situation was particularly reflected at the Marienfelde factory where quite a number of 1-ton electric-powered delivery vehicles were produced for a Berlin concern.

The Marienfelde factory also became well-known for its fire engines, particularly a design produced in 1907 following very intensive research.

The year 1907 was also a landmark for another reason; it saw Wilhelm Maybach leaving Daimler. He left the company having established it as the leading European contender in truck manufacture with the three main factories at Cannstatt, Marienfelde and Wiener-Neustadt and with strong overseas representation, particularly in England. There, the Milnes-Daimler concern, which was based in the Tottenham Court Road, in the heart of London, had gone from strength to strength selling vehicles for a wide variety of uses from tippers to tower wagons and from ordinary load-carriers to purpose-built vans for the Royal Mail.

The main works of Benz in the early-1900s was still at the Mannheim factory where the company had started in 1886. However, the Benz company was looking for expansion and its interest centred on the Suddeutschen Automobielfabrik GmbH SAF at Gaggenau. Gaggenau is not far from Baden-Baden in the Black Forest. Suddeutschen Automobielfabrik was formed there in 1905. The company was really a continuation of Bergmanns Industriewerken Gaggenau, established in 1893, which had built its first car in 1895.

This is the first automotive diesel to be built by Daimler-Benz. It was made at the Mannheim factory and was installed in 1923 in a 5-tonne payload vehicle. It had a maximum power output of 45 bhp at 1,000 rpm.

SAF, as it was known, quickly established a sound engineering reputation for both its cars and its trucks and this drew the attention of Benz & Cie in Mannheim. The result, in 1907, was a joint working agreement which led to the production of buses and goods vehicles of up to 6 tons gross weight before a complete takeover by Benz in 1910 and the formation of Benzwerke Gaggenau GmbH. Unusually, the SAF works built a forward-control truck at this time, whereas the rest of the German industry was building bonneted models.

The installation of the first Daimler-Benz diesel was in this bonneted truck of 1923, a 5-tonner designated the K3.

From the time it was taken over the factory concentrated on the production of trucks, buses and special vehicles, a role which has not been lost for today the Gaggenau plant is responsible for Unimog production.

It was here, of course, that the first diesel truck was built in September 1923, and it also became the centre of truck production when Daimler and Benz amalgamated in 1926.

It was in the Marienfelde factory, however, that Daimler developed its diesel engines, the factory first taking on this role in 1910. These were not automotive diesels, although obviously there was a technological influence exerted on later automotive diesel engine designs.

As indicated earlier, the Marienfelde plant, from its early days, built quite a number of military vehicles, a role which was to continue up to the end of the First World War. These included 4 × 4s for civilian as well as military use, with 60-bhp engines. Perhaps the most important of the 1914-18 designs was the 3-ton chain-driven model which strangely, perhaps, had glass side and front windscreens. They were ordered in quantity by the German Army. The equivalent Benz 3-tonner built at Gaggenau was almost equally popular. Both had four-cylinder engines of 37 bhp.

In the 1912-14 period when, as in France and England, there was a subsidy policy in Germany on vehicles for potential military duties, Marienfelde built heavier chain and prop-shaft driven 4 × 2 designs. These were 4/5-tonners with 45-bhp engines and all, of course, still fitted with wooden spoked wheels and solid rubber tyres.

Austro-Daimler, besides producing the heavy-duty tractor units mentioned earlier, predictably built a number of special designs for wartime use. They included 4 × 4 mobile winches for observer balloons and 4 × 4 recovery vehicles and an articulating field gun in which the conventional front end of the vehicle with single axle was employed with the field gun's axle and wheels acting as the vehicle's rear wheels. This had a light 15-bhp air-cooled engine, as had a light multi-purpose 1-ton 4 × 2 truck built at the same time.

The years that followed the war were difficult ones throughout Europe, but nowhere more so than in Germany. Economic conditions were bad and did not start to improve

The first Daimler-Benz automotive diesel-engined vehicle with bonnet covers removed and showing the distinctive cylinder-head configuration of the four-cylinder power unit.

A Bosch injection pump was used to fuel the first Daimler-Benz diesel engine.

until the 1930s. It was, however, in this period that both Daimler and Benz moved towards the use of diesel engines in their vehicles with Daimler at the Marienfelde factory relying on a design in which the fuel was injected into the cylinder by air pressure. This air-pressure system had already proved successful in much larger engines for generating set applications including a six-cylinder unit producing 380 bhp at 1,700 rpm.

However, Marienfelde applied its expertise to small engines as well, initially for agricultural machinery use. It was not until 1921 that three four-cylinder engines of 110 mm bore and 150 mm stroke producing 40 bhp at 1,000 rpm were built and one of these, fitted with a supercharger, was installed in a bus. After successful road-testing, similar engines were installed in trucks and a diesel-powered general haulage vehicle and a 3-ton tipper were exhibited at the Berlin Show in October 1923.

Built from 1932 to 1936, this diesel-powered type L 3000 had a payload of 3 tonnes.

At Benz, meanwhile, a 30-bhp pre-combustion-chamber diesel engine design had been developed from the basic concept of a man with the picturesque name of Prosper L'Orange in the 1900s. With agricultural machinery and automotive applications in mind, the Benz Stationary Engine Department was transformed into the Motor Works which came to be known as MWN. That happened in April 1922. Tests in agricultural machinery proved so successful that it was decided, in March 1923, that 100 engines of this type should be built. One of these was fitted in a 5-ton Benz truck which had its world premiere at the Amsterdam Show of 1924. Designated the OB2, it had a bore of 125 mm and a stroke of 180 mm. Initially, Benz injection pumps and nozzles were fitted, but these were soon replaced with Bosch units.

By this time, Daimler and Benz were co-operating actively with one another and, in fact, as a result of a preliminary amalgamation in 1924, Daimler's combustion system was dropped in favour of the Benz concept.

The companies were only a step away from full amalgamation, an event which took place in 1926. Daimler-Benz AG was the new name given to the company with its headquarters and a new central design department based at Stuttgart-Untertürkheim.

A main outward sign of this merger was the amalgamation of the Daimler company's trademark — the three-pointed star — with that of the laurel wreath of Benz.

The German automotive industry in the 1920s was in a very severely depressed state and the amalgamation of Daimler and Benz was very largely a recipe for survival. Rationalization of production was also essential. The Marienfelde factory was perhaps the hardest hit by the recession and was forced to switch entirely to repair work. In fact, things did not pick up for Marienfelde until the 1930s and production was not resumed there until 1934 when the plant started building cross-country vehicles and engines.

Things were only a degree less difficult at Gaggenau and

The L 2000, originally produced in 1931, was one of the main designs built in the 1930s. It was powered by a 55-bhp four-cylinder diesel engine.

A gas-powered version of the L 3000 produced between 1941 and 1945.

Fitted with a 120-bhp diesel engine, this L 4500 model with a 4½ tonnes payload is seen here with a tank body for fire-fighting use. It was built in 1944.

Mannheim and it was decided to limit production to three basic designs — a 1½-tonner, a 2/3-tonner and a 5-tonner, the last also being built as a bus chassis.

In 1931 came what was known as the L-series with the designations of L 1500, L 3000 and L 5000. The numbers reflected the payloads in kilogrammes. All were offered with diesel engines and petrol engines as the option. The L 1500 had a four-cylinder 45-bhp power unit, the L 3000 a 70-bhp four-cylinder engine and the L 5000 a six-cylinder 85-bhp initially and later a 110-bhp unit.

A powerful 4-tonner (the L 4000 with a 100-bhp six-cylinder diesel engine), a 2-tonner (the L 2000 with a four-cylinder 55-bhp diesel engine) and a 6½-tonner (the L 6500, with a six-cylinder diesel) were subsequently added to the range.

In 1932 Daimler-Benz built and sold 2,000 diesel vehicles, and such was the development from that point on that 1935 saw 10,000 constructed.

A feature of the six-wheelers as early as 1927 was hub reduction in the rear axles. Cross-country model G3a 4 × 4s and heavy-duty tractor units were also produced in the 1930s. All these vehicles were bonneted designs and forward-control designs were not due to appear until the years following the Second World War.

Production of the standard German Army truck and the L-series and G-series models, adapted for military use, took Daimler-Benz through the difficult and often hazardous years of the 1939-45 war.

Chapter 2

Postwar reconstruction

After the Second World War Daimler-Benz had almost to start from scratch to rebuild its organization. As the board of Daimler-Benz said in 1945, the company, as a result of air attacks, had 'practically ceased to exist'. The exception to some degree was Mannheim. The Americans are alleged to have left this alone in the latter days of the war as they had it designated as a major truck repair centre for their own vehicles once it was occupied. And that is exactly what happened.

The effects of the war on the Marienfelde works were especially severe and it was not until the summer of 1950 that it resumed the manufacture of diesel engines for installation in generating sets and boats and for industrial equipment.

It was almost equally as bad at every other factory of Daimler-Benz, but recovery elsewhere was faster. The first to get back into operation was Gaggenau, which had in fact been destroyed in 1944. And it was done with a totally new vehicle! This was the multi-purpose Unimog, which went into production in 1948, the factory having come back into limited operation in September 1945. The Unimog not only served as an agricultural tractor but, with its 4 × 4 characteristics and robust design, it was put to all kinds of uses on and off the road. It has since become one of the most important products out of Gaggenau — and out of Daimler-Benz for that matter.

Daimler-Benz's first annual report after the war makes fascinating reading. It is also a rather sad document for it includes in the opening section a tribute to the 2,483 Daimler-Benz workers who died in the war in the forces and in air-raids and the 816 who were registered as 'missing'. It is, however, a tribute to the workforce of that time that they surmounted overwhelming problems to get the plants limping back into operation.

Mannheim concentrated on production of 3-tonners, all normal-control designs, building 747 of them there in the period from May 1945 when the war ended to the end of the year. A total of 1,497 was built in 1946 at a production rate which varied from 37 to 271 a month. This rate went up to between 110 and 300 units a month in 1947 and 2,001 were built in that year, a figure which was to be substantially bettered in 1948; the 1948 report reveals that no less than 1,750 were ordered in the period up to June 20 of that year.

Meanwhile, in November 1945, the Unterturkheim and Sindelfingen plants had been allocated to produce small parcels vans, pickups, personnel carriers and ambulances. A total of 214 of these were built in 1946 and 1,045 in the following year; then the factory really started to recover, for in the following six months to June 20, 1948, a total of 1,304 units was made.

Gaggenau, building 5-tonne trucks, seems to have been slower in building up its unit production rate. A total of 290 5-tonners were built in 1945, a figure which went up to 522 in 1946, but fell to 403 in 1947. To June 20, 1948, however, 342 vehicles were built, including a number of buses.

The workforce of the whole group in this period rose from

One of the first vehicles to go into production in the period immediately following World War 2 was the Unimog. This one, fitted with a four-cylinder 25-bhp engine, was one of the early examples built in 1949.

12,849 in 1945 to 22,548 in 1948. At this stage of the group's development, the traditional main manufacturing centres were at Unterturkheim, Sindelfingen (the car factory before the war), Mannheim, Gaggenau and Berlin-Marienfelde.

Recovery was still a long way off in 1948 and shortage of every kind of raw material was not made easier by legislation in Germany. As has been implied, the occupation forces dictated the types of vehicle which Daimler-Benz could produce. Control Commission requirements restricted German manufacturers to the production of two-axled goods vehicles. The building of multi-wheelers was banned, although the operation of lorries and drawbar trailers (sometimes two trailers were towed) provided the required payload levels. This restriction was not lifted until 1951 and was obviously an inhibiting factor.

When Federal German laws replaced the Control Commission requirements, the state-owned Federal Railways exerted a strong influence to restrict road transport. Safeguards to boost the railway role in domestic transport were built into the laws governing the weight, dimensions and other characteristics of commercial vehicles. This was to have an inhibiting impact, which still continues. However, certain other requirements like minimum power-to-weight ratios were to have a dramatic influence on shaping European heavy vehicle design in the years to come.

In spite of the problems, reconstruction and re-equipping of the factories forged ahead and new and improved models began to appear. The British had inspired and encouraged the establishment of Hanover as a centre for exhibiting German products — who would have thought it was to become the

The first range of Mercedes-Benz goods vehicles to be developed in the years following World War 2 was the type L 3250, shown here in chassis form. It was a 3½-tonner with a six-cylinder 90-bhp diesel engine and was first shown at the Hanover Fair in 1949.

The L 5000 5-tonner, shown here with a tank body, was the larger of the two models built by Daimler-Benz from 1949 onwards. Like the L 3250, it made its debut at the 1949 Hanover Fair.

world's leading exhibition ground — and the years of accelerating recovery (1948 to 1951) saw a number of model introductions there by D-B.

The key to the start of this recovery was in the currency reform implemented in Germany in June 1948, the establishment of the first Federal German Government in 1949 and the creation of government policies — due to be highly successful — towards re-establishing German industry.

The appearance of the type 170S passenger car in May 1949 tended, perhaps, to overshadow the fact that it was the goods vehicle activities which were contributing the major part towards the country's resurgence.

It was in this period that the high-power-to-weight-ratio principle was established which was to characterize German vehicles in the next 30 years.

One of the most popular Mercedes vehicles of the 1950s, the Type LA 312 shown here was built from 1953 through to 1961.

Introduced in 1951, the L 6600K bonneted 6.6-tonner was a popular vehicle for construction work. This example is fitted with a three-way tipping body.

Limited in the size of vehicles as they were, it is interesting to speculate whether the designers of that period were looking to the time when much heavier lorries would be permitted. Then, of course, D-B would be ready with suitable power units. This is what eventually happened. The success of the range introduced was largely founded on the development of a six-cylinder diesel engine.

At Hanover in 1949, a new model range was announced with this diesel engine rated to produce 90 bhp. This started with the L 3250 which, with this level of engine power, not surprisingly became known as 'the fast truck' because of its performance characteristics. It became the L 3500 in 1950. Note the continuation of the simple designation system; the number indicated the payload in kilogrammes. There was a medium-weight vehicle in the range, the L 5000 (payload 5 tonnes) powered by a 120-bhp diesel and the heavy-duty L 6600 (payload 6.6 tonnes) with a 145-bhp diesel built largely at Mannheim.

Not many Mercedes-Benz articulated tractor units were built in the early-1950s. This bonneted LS 3500 model was designed to offer a payload of 7.5 tonnes.

The new models — all normal-control units, incidentally — were not introduced entirely painlessly. Statistics reveal a big drop in production for the Mannheim works in the June-July period of 1950 as they were phased-in, but from August onwards they jumped to a level 50 per cent up on the previous high and stayed there right up to the end of 1951, when the next leap forward came.

Meanwhile, production at Gaggenau was concentrated on 5-tonners. The increase in production there rocketed from 623 in 1948 to 1,694 in 1950, a year in which the 6.6-tonner was put into production alongside the 5-tonner.

In its report for 1949 to 1950 (the second of the financial reports after the war), D-B compared the 1939 prices with those for 1950; the 1950 versions cost 41 per cent more than those of 1939. Moreover the rate of the deutschemark against the dollar had fallen, and this made exports difficult.

The first purpose-built van from Daimler-Benz in the 1950s was the L 319. As the picture on the next page makes clear, a feature was the relatively easy access to the vehicle afforded to the driver.

The LP 333 twin-steer, six-wheeler shown here was one of the first forward-control models to be built by Daimler-Benz after World War 2. It was launched in 1958.

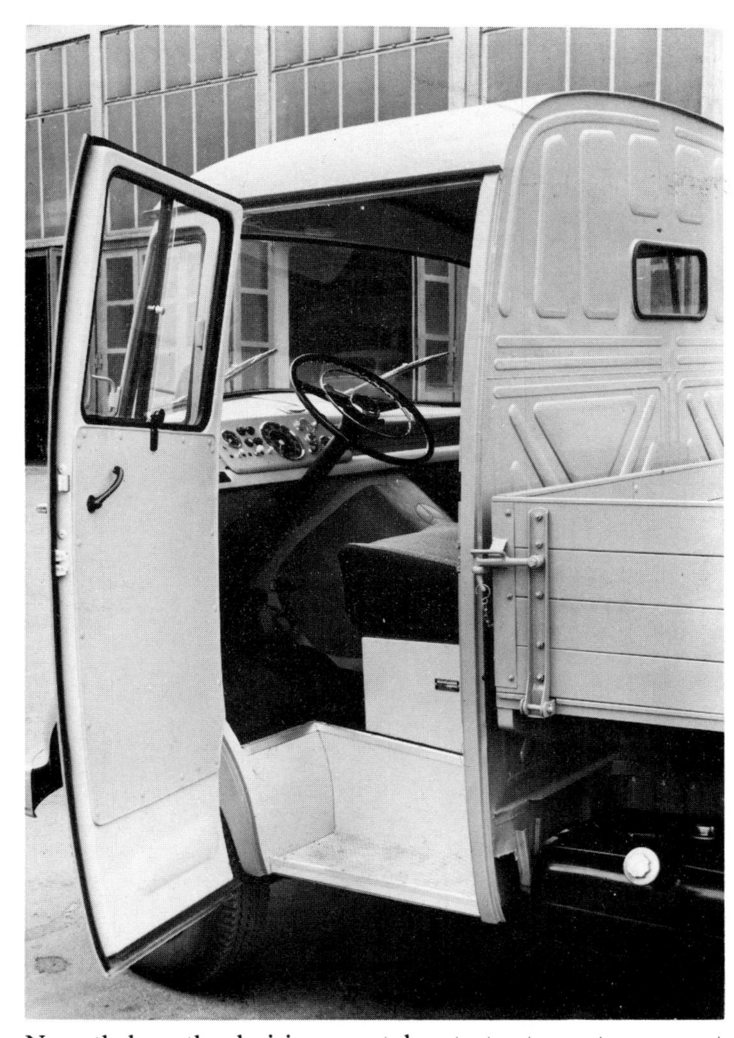

Nevertheless, the decision was taken to try to capture export markets, and a determined move in 1950 met with tremendous success. In that year Daimler-Benz exported vehicles — mainly private cars — to a value of DM 66 million to over 50 countries. The measure of this achievement is reflected by the fact that in 1949 exports had totalled just DM 6 million.

By the end of 1951, it was apparent that the main problems of the postwar period had been overcome and the company was moving ahead. Mannheim built 8,758 3½-tonners in that year and 890 buses, whilst Gaggenau constructed 2,382 5-tonners and 6.6-tonners as well as 239 heavy-duty buses.

This, of course, was the year when Daimler and Benz celebrated the 25th anniversary of their amalgamation. Appropriately, it was a good year financially for the company, providing a springboard for its expansion in the 1950s and beyond.

It was in 1954 that the model designation system was changed, the payload-linked system being altered to one in which the development number of the vehicle was employed. The first model to reflect this was the L 315, which had a 7-tonnes payload. It continued the postwar trend in that it was a normal-control (bonneted) design. In fact, the first postwar forward-control model, the LP 315, was not produced until 1955; this had a similar specification to the L 315 save for the cab. The P in the designation stands for 'Pullman', a German term for forward control. It was on this model that Daimler-Benz introduced an exhaust brake as standard equipment.

The introduction of these vehicles marked the second phase of Daimler-Benz's postwar truck development. It broke away from the three-model programme which characterized the 10 years from 1945 to 1955. The next model to break away from the stereotyped pattern was the LP 319/319D, a speedy forward-control light delivery vehicle which had a payload of 1¾ tonnes.

However, it was still in the lighter-weight class and it was not until later the same year — 1956 — that changes occurred which were to have a significant influence on Daimler-Benz and to mould the future model programme. These were changes in the German construction requirements and dimension and weight limits. The outcome of the changes in the legal requirements was a move to three-axled rigid vehicles in one direction and lighter two-axled rigids in the other.

To meet the regulations, a twin-steer three-axled design, the

Bonneted tractor units like this LS 329 model employed by a brewery were still the rule rather than the exception in Germany in the late-1950s and early-1960s. This design was built from 1957 to 1962.

The robust character of the chassis can be seen in this photograph of an LAK 329/37 intended as a bonneted vehicle for tipping-vehicle and ready-mixed concrete applications. It was built from 1957 to 1962.

The fitment of a forward-control cab on the LP 321 was considered a revolutionary move by Daimler-Benz in 1958. Its introduction, however, was to set the pattern for the future as forward-control rapidly took over from bonneted models from this point on.

LP 333, was evolved and built for operation at 16 tonnes gross weight. It made its debut in 1958 and was also constructed as a tractive unit for articulated vehicle operation at a gross combination weight of 24 tonnes when coupled to a semi-trailer. There was plenty of power for the OM 326 diesel engine produced 200 bhp, reflecting the fact that a minimum power-to-weight ratio of 6 bhp per tonne had become a feature of West Germany's truck construction laws. This adoption of what then was considered to be a high power-to-weight ratio was to prove of immense benefit to Daimler-Benz in international competition in the years to follow.

Production continued to rise at both the Mannheim and the Gaggenau plants. At the former, total build in 1955 was 18,930 trucks and buses. Of these, 13,047 were the 4½-tonners, against 3,993 3½-tonners and 1,990 buses. At Gaggenau, production in the same year at 10,698 comprised 1,582 6-tonners, 4,083 7-tonners and 306 heavy-duty buses, along with 4,727 Unimogs.

In 1956, annual production of 3.5 and 4.5-tonne trucks had reached 24,335 at the Mannheim works whilst at Gaggenau the lines producing the 6-tonners, 6.5-tonners, 7-tonners and 8.5-tonners hit a level of 5,969. These were mainly 6-tonners and 7-tonners, for the other two weights did not come on stream until October in the case of the 6.5-tonner and September for the 8.5-tonne vehicle. The fact that the company had been able to extend its weight range was, however, already proving significant.

Gaggenau also built 4,999 Unimogs in the same year and, with a further 5,940 in 1957, passed the 20,000 mark for diesel-powered Unimogs from the time they were introduced. Otherwise, however, 1957 was not such a good year for Daimler-Benz for truck production fell at both the Mannheim and the Gaggenau works. But a boom year was to follow, at least for the Mannheim works, where the production of 3.5 to 5.5-tonners jumped by some 10,000 units. The pace then continued to quicken, especially when, in 1959, the company added three new models to its range, but more about these in a moment.

Not quite a bonneted model and not quite a 'cab-over', the Mercedes L 322 semi-forward-control design was developed in the 1950s, but did not come on to the market in volume until 1961.

The end of the decade saw the manufacturing figures still rising. In 1960, production at Mannheim hit a record 42,117 goods vehicles and 4,331 buses. An interesting aspect of the production statistics is that 19,650 of these goods vehicles were listed as complete vehicles, but in kit form for export. This was a remarkable figure for vehicle kit production had only started at the Mannheim works in August 1959 and a relatively modest 5,310 sets were produced that year. The 1959 figure reflected the introduction of a successful export model, the LP 327, a 7.5-tonner which formed part of a new model programme unveiled in March 1959 and also including the L/LP 322, a 6-tonner, and the L/LP 337, a vehicle rated at 7.3 tonnes.

Unimog production at Gaggenau also rose steeply in 1960 to 9,450 units, compared with 6,766 in the previous year. Truck production also increased there with the 6-tonne to 7.5-tonne category rising to 3,385 from 2,565 in 1959 and the over-7.5-tonne category moving up marginally from 4,231 to 4,560. The construction of truck kits for export started at Gaggenau in 1960.

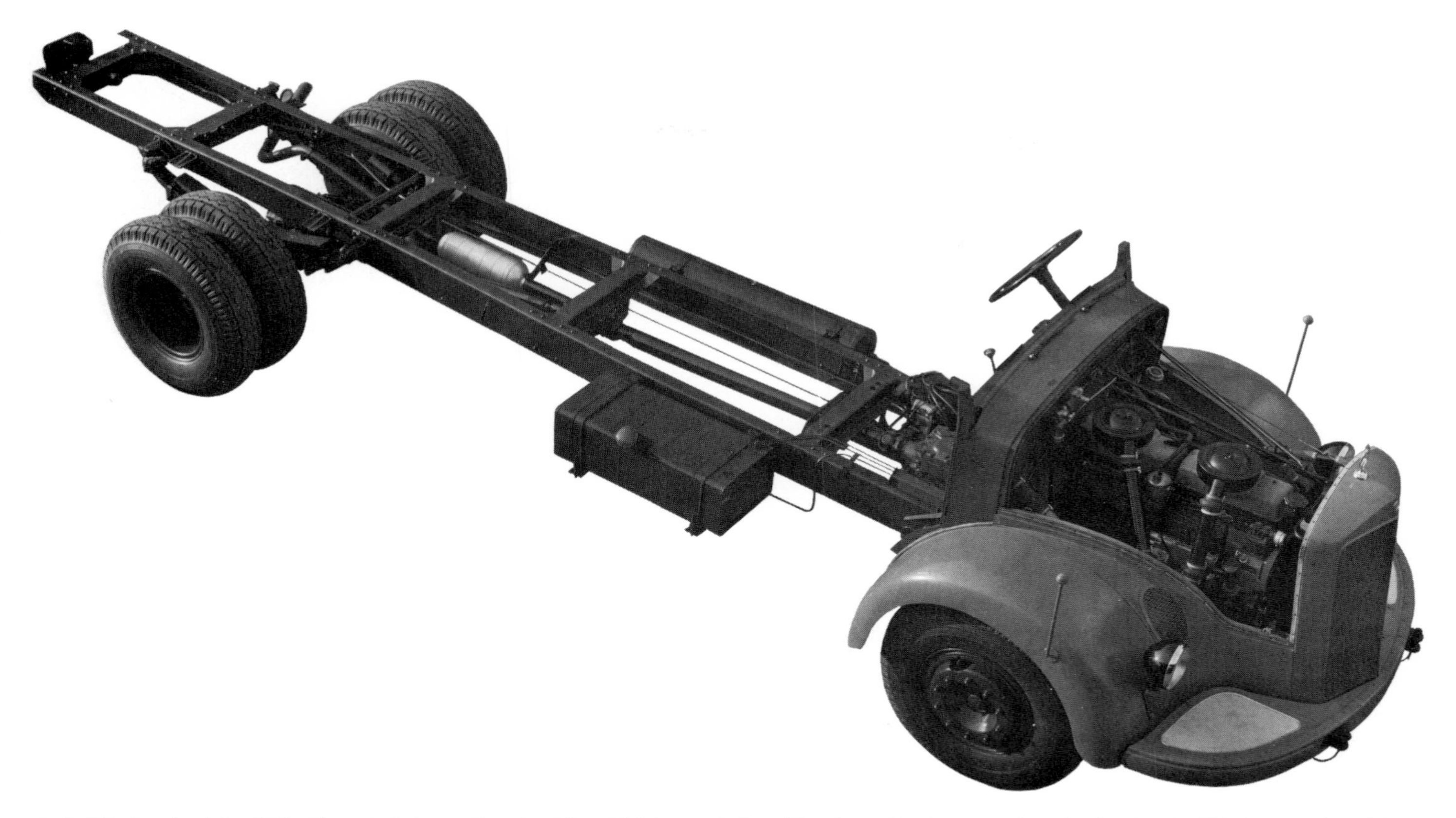

An L 315 chassis of the 1950s. The relatively small payload for which it was designed is reflected in the somewhat slender chassis. This bonneted model was built at the Gaggenau factory. The chassis was also available in forward-control form.

Meanwhile, the type L 319 1.75-tonner remained the only commercial vehicle to be built at the Stuttgart Unterturkheim plant and 8,209 of these were built in 1960. Together, the three plants built 72,960 commercial vehicles in 1960, including buses, and the factories could not increase production any further without expansion.

The signs that Daimler-Benz was gathering momentum as a major vehicle producer were there in other ways in the late-1950s. One outward sign was the construction in 1958 of the 14-storey administration building. It was also establishing and consolidating an embryo empire overseas — moves which are dealt with separately in the chapter on overseas activities.

There were other developments as well. Unterturkheim is the centre for Daimler-Benz's vehicle testing programmes and

A pickup version of the L 319 of 1956 with a payload of 1¾ tonnes.

it was there in 1955 that the first moves were made to establish a self-contained test track. The emphasis initially was placed on a high-speed track for cars and it was not until the late-1960s that it was expanded to offer the elaborate facilities affording the opportunity to test virtually every feature of every type of vehicle produced by the company.

So, here was this formidable company with the 1960s ahead, not just up to full production at all its truck plants, but bursting at the seams, and equipped with a thoroughly modern headquarters with sound facilities. The company also had a superb profits record so there were no financial problems. In retrospect, as they say, 'they couldn't fail' because it was at this time that the whole German industry was given a tremendous boost by the relaxation of restrictive weight laws.

The permitted gross weight of two-axled vehicles was raised from 12 to 16 tonnes and the single rear axle weight to 10 tonnes. For articulated vehicles and lorries and trailers a new maximum weight limit was introduced of 32 tonnes. Daimler-Benz was quick to respond to the changed situation.

Chapter 3

Expanding the manufacturing base

In 1960 it was realized that the two main Daimler-Benz commercial vehicle plants at Mannheim and Gaggenau had reached their full capacity. They were building about 130 medium and heavy-duty trucks a day and were close to their working limit in terms of space and workforce.

A major plan was accordingly drawn up for the whole of the company's commercial vehicle operations. The momentous decision was taken to build a new works and rationalize totally manufacturing operations at Mannheim and Gaggenau, a policy which was subsequently followed at all other plants.

Daimler-Benz looked for a suitable site and eventually selected one in a development area at Woerth where the local authorities were offering attractive incentives. In November 1960, the contract was signed to purchase 150 hectares (470 acres) of land and almost immediately work began on the construction of what was to be Daimler-Benz's main medium-duty and heavy-duty truck assembly plant.

This move was perhaps the most significant — in production terms — in the postwar era for Daimler-Benz, for Woerth has proved the springboard for Daimler-Benz's leap ahead in commercial vehicle markets. Naturally, it took a little time to plan, construct and equip the new plant and, when it eventually opened in 1965, it triggered the vehicle expansion programmes of the late-1960s and 1970s.

The establishment of the operation at Woerth formed part of the general strategy of Daimler-Benz which had proved itself successful in the car sector; specialization of particular factories on certain tasks.

This policy was to result in all medium and heavy truck assembly and cab production being concentrated at Woerth with the two main truck works at Mannheim and Gaggenau switching to major truck components (engines, gearboxes and axles).

Mannheim was designated as the location of a new foundry and engine plant. Construction of this began in 1962 and it was opened in 1965. The foundry started making the crankcases and cylinder-heads for commercial vehicle engines and also fulfilled part of the casting requirements of the Unterturkheim car plant. Capital expenditure was directed primarily to the production of chassis parts and the expansion of engine manufacturing operations. Mannheim started building all truck and bus engines at this time, eventually constructing the highly successful 400 series of vee-engines for medium and heavy-duty trucks and buses introduced in 1970. The production of the 400 series engine was stepped up within months of its introduction as axle manufacturing for light and medium-weight trucks was transferred elsewhere.

Since the Mannheim plant began operations, there have obviously been changes and improvements, which are still taking place. Just one of the significant developments was the adoption of the cold-box process in a new core shop for crankcases in 1978. The year 1975 was also particularly notable for Mannheim with the manufacture of its millionth

An LK 2624 export tipper model built at Kassel until 1980.

An 'on-line' photograph of the Bremen light van plant in 1979 showing a body being positioned over a chassis before mounting.

diesel engine.

When Woerth was opened in 1965 the first vehicles it built were LP 608 models, 800 chassis being constructed in that first year. In addition, the Mannheim factories constructed 26,851 medium-weights and Gaggenau 9,630 heavies. The Duesseldorf plant produced 15,300 light vans and pickups.

These are important figures to bear in mind having regard to the subsequent statistics when heavy and medium-weight production was transferred from Gaggenau and Mannheim in 1968. At Woerth, in that year, Daimler-Benz built 41,957 medium-weights and heavies (6 tonnes upwards).

The move to Woerth was not only the prelude to expansion of its own range, for it was not long after it had gone into operation that Daimler-Benz acquired one of its biggest rivals in the form of the commercial vehicle operation of the Rheinstahl group — which included the Hanomag and Henschel brand names. However, before looking at the impact of the Hanomag-Henschel acquisition it is relevant to review the situation at the Duesseldorf plant.

In the 1950s, the Duesseldorf plant was part of Auto-Union, producing about 60,000 DKW private cars annually. When Auto-Union concentrated its operations at Ingolstadt, the Duesseldorf-Derendorf plant was acquired in 1962 by Daimler-Benz.

The main production line for heavy trucks at the Woerth factory, construction of which began in 1961 on a 150-hectare site.

After its takeover, the plant was put to a wide variety of tasks until, in 1969, it was allocated to van and minibus production and the manufacture of steering units. As a result, in the 1980s, Duesseldorf manufactures all Mercedes vans and minibuses in the 3.5 to 6.5-tonne gvw range as well as all steering units for Mercedes passenger cars and commercial vehicles.

The main model produced initially at Duesseldorf was the 319, which was succeeded in 1967 by the model 309 and in 1968 the 310 was added. In 1965 production was around 15,000 units, a figure which rose to approximately 30,000 by 1980.

The restructuring of the Duesseldorf plant took place in five stages from 1970 to 1978. The same thing happened at Duesseldorf as at Woerth in that the re-organization was aimed at producing component families in only one plant.

First came the concentration of steering unit manufacture in the areas vacated by the transfer of axle and engine production and in newly built shops. Vehicle assembly operations were then installed in an enlarged building formerly used for steering and gearshift manufacture.

This was followed by the re-organization and streamlining of bodyshell production using the space vacated by assembly. Accompanying this was the construction of a new vehicle delivery centre on a site north of the plant.

Finally, the parts painting operations were re-arranged and

The heart of Daimler-Benz — the Stuttgart-Unterturkheim complex, showing part of the test track in the foreground.

Daimler-Benz's main truck plant at Woerth is the biggest in Europe. It employs 9,000 people and is strategically positioned commercially, being adjacent to the Rhine harbour and having excellent road and rail connections.

a new large-scale paint shop was constructed (completed in 1979) employing modern painting techniques, including electrophoretic dip priming.

During this period of development in the 1970s, practically all production units, storage areas and workshops in Duesseldorf were re-organized and updated at a cost of DM 200 million to create a concentrated and rationalized manufacturing process.

In the 1980s, apart from manufacturing the 3.5 to 6.5-tonne van range, Duesseldorf also makes the steering for every vehicle made by D-B from mechanical passenger car steering units to power steering for heavy trucks.

By the end of the 1970s, the Duesseldorf vehicle range consisted of 16 basic models and 177 different variants of buses and vans, plus some 550 special equipment items. The vans were offered in seven different weight classes with 3.5, 4, 4.6, 5.2, 5.6, 5.9 and 6.5 tonnes gvw. They were available as box-type vans with various cargo space dimensions (interior height and length), as pickups — also with crew cab, as chassis for special bodies and in various different special versions, for example, for fire brigades and ambulance services. Four engine outputs from 60 to 130 bhp were available for the Duesseldorf range.

Back now to the Hanomag-Henschel takeover. Hanomag-Henschel Fahrzeugbau AG, of Hanover, was a company formed by Daimler-Benz from Hanomag of Hanover and F. Henschel Sohn of Kassel immediately on takeover on March 1, 1969. Hanomag itself had taken over in 1963 the light van and truck (1 tonne to 3 tonnes) operation of Vidal & Sohn, Tempowerke, manufacturers of the Matador and Wiking marques of light transporter. The light transporters built by Hanomag were unconventional in that they featured an unusual form of independent front suspension and front-wheel drive.

The takeover was important in many ways for D-B, but in particular it opened the light van market sector to the company. In 1968 Hanomag-Henschel built 19,410 light transporters, 14,663 medium-weights and 4,201 heavies, a total of 38,274 vehicles.

In the first year after takeover Daimler-Benz pushed this total up by 26.6 per cent to 48,373 units out of a total

Unimogs and MB-tracs on the assembly line at the Gaggenau plant.

Transporters, pickup trucks and small bus chassis in the gross weight category from 3.5 to 6.6 tonnes on the production line at Duesseldorf.

The Bremen light van plant from the air.

The Daimler-Benz headquarters building at Stuttgart-Unterturkheim, where the company's famous museum is also located.

production of 170,527 Daimler-Benz commercial vehicles (24,423 in overseas plants).

D-B commented at this time that in order to remain internationally competitive it had become increasingly necessary, from both the economic and the technological standpoints, to manufacture more vehicles. 'Having regard to the production capacity already available in Germany it did not appear expedient to create still further new capacity, but to merge existing plants and their workforces into a rational and efficient union.' The absorption of Hanomag-Henschel had made it possible fully to utilize existing production and sales potential by standardization of important parts and assemblies to produce vehicles in economic and competitive quantities.

Referring in 1970 to the extraordinarily wide range of models offered, D-B commented that standardization of the many types of vehicles produced was difficult because of the special requirements of the various export markets and different local vehicle legislation requirements. In the case of certain models, a large number of different versions was essential. This made it necessary to standardize parts and assemblies where possible. A reflection of this was the establishment of the central axle works at Kassel for both Mercedes-Benz and Hanomag-Henschel vehicles.

The Daimler factory at Stuttgart-Unterturkheim in 1911.

An engine test cell at the Mannheim engine plant.

Cab manufacture in the early days of Woerth. The photograph reveals the degree of automation employed, even in those days, in cab construction.

When the Kassel works of the Hanomag-Henschel Group was acquired as a result of the D-B takeover, it was quickly welded into the Daimler-Benz structure, being designated as a components plant within a year of takeover.

The integration of Kassel with Daimler-Benz's other operation was a continuing process not finally completed until 1978. In the 1980s it is believed to be the biggest commercial vehicle axle plant in Europe, producing about 1,600 commercial vehicle axles a day.

A late-1970s development at Kassel was the decision to introduce volume manufacture of axles for the cross-country vehicle built with Steyr-Daimler-Puch of Austria. Kassel has also taken over axle gear production from Gaggenau.

Cab construction at Woerth was enlarged in 1969 to enable daily production to be increased from 205 to 260 vehicles, the highest rate of increase being achieved in respect of heavy trucks.

Until the Hanomag-Henschel takeover, Daimler-Benz did not have an interest in really light vans and the range began at 4 tonnes with the Duesseldorf products. From this point on, however, light transporters were to play a major role.

By 1970, production of vehicles of up to 4 tonnes had been pushed up to 32,523 and in 1971 the figure moved to 35,524, in 1972 to 47,447 and by 1980 it totalled 53,353.

Initially, the light van models were built both in Bremen and Hamburg, production being at first rationalized between the two factories, with the Hamburg factory concentrating on flats and pickups and Bremen on vans.

Hanomag-Henschel middleweights were also built at Bremen, but the Hanomag-Henschel line was competitive with that of D-B, so although the two lines were continued for a while Hanomag-Henschel production was gradually run down and the last few vehicles were badged Mercedes. At Kassel much the same thing happened, but with the D-B engined chassis cabbed with the Henschel unit before finally the whole vehicle became Mercedes.

The production facilities at Hamburg and Kassel were old, but the premises at Bremen were good, so the decision was taken to concentrate light van production there, introducing D-B production methods and facilities, and the new Bremen

Component design and testing is carried out at the central development centre in Stuttgart.

range was produced there from 1977. Meanwhile, the Hamburg factory was gradually switched to parts manufacture for trucks and cars.

In the 1980s, the lightest vehicles produced by Daimler-Benz are built at Sebaldsbruck, in Bremen. These vans, in the 2.55 to 3.5-tonne gvw categories and comprising the 207 D 308 models, went into production there in 1977 in what at one time had been the Borgward car factory. It was acquired in 1961 by the Hanomag company and taken over by D-B in 1969 on the acquisition of the Rheinstahl Group. After the takeover, Bremen built the P 14 van until the new range was introduced in 1977.

Over 50,000 Bremen vans are now produced annually, in the form of pickups and box vans, or as crew buses, with the option of either a 2.4-litre diesel or a 2.3-litre petrol engine. They are available in three wheelbases and there are more than 200 body variations.

Bremen, however, is also a car plant and to make room for an increase in car production the capacity of the plant has been expanded, and van production will eventually be taken over by other commercial vehicle plants.

As Daimler-Benz moved into the 1980s its commercial vehicle production locations continued to be controlled from the D-B head office at Stuttgart-Unterturkheim, where the planning and design division, backed by the research and development department, mapped out the future for D-B's truck activities. Prototype testing continued at the test track first established there in the early-1970s. The Unterturkheim plant remained, as it always had been, a car plant, as did Sindelfingen.

Woerth continued as the principal truck factory with a daily capacity of more than 300 vehicles assembling all trucks over 6 tonnes other than semi-forward-control models. It was also the location of the central spare parts store for commercial vehicles.

Duesseldorf remained the centre for assembling all commercial vehicles between 3.5 and 6.4 tonnes, including small buses. It also was the main centre for steering gear manufacture of all types. Bremen remained the production location for light vans (and the T-range estate cars).

Gaggenau continued to make the Unimog and MB trac ranges, as well as transmissions and planetary gear hub-reduction axles for the heavy-duty trucks assembled at Woerth. It was the location of the press shop for cabs for the commercial vehicle ranges and Unimogs.

Mannheim, the centre of commercial vehicle engine production, included the main foundry making the more difficult castings for both commercial vehicle and car engines. It was also the main location for bus and coach production.

Kassel remained as the main centre for axle production and for the assembly of semi-forward-control trucks.

Berlin-Marienfelde, Bad Homburg, in Frankfurt, and Harburg, in Hamburg, continued to make components for cars and commercial vehicles, with the Berlin factory, for example, specializing in crankshafts and gears and exchange engines for commercial vehicles and Frankfurt for valves and valve timing gears.

Chapter 4

The 1960s: Broadening the product range

The progress made by Daimler-Benz in the 1950s owed a great deal to steady demand from municipal authorities, still short of transport after the war, and the construction industry.

However, the pattern of domestic requirements was changing with the municipal market diminishing — relatively — in importance. There was a growing need for vehicles to operate internationally throughout Europe and, later, for container carrying — bigger, heavier, vehicles.

These were some of the influences which led the German Federal Government in 1960 to implement changes in its construction requirements. These resulted in two-axled vehicles being permitted to operate at a maximum weight of 16 tonnes instead of 12 tonnes, with 10 tonnes on the rear axle instead of 8 tonnes. The weight for on-highway, three-axled vehicles was raised to 22 tonnes and for similar vehicles operating off-highway to 26 tonnes. There was a major change for articulated vehicles, the maximum combination weight rising to 32 tonnes gcw.

First of the Mercedes four-wheeler models to meet the new weight laws was the LP 334, a vehicle constructed at Gaggenau and adapted from an existing export model built for operation at 19 tonnes gross weight with a 13-tonne rear axle.

With higher weights, the power-to-weight ratio law, referred to in Chapter 2, exerted an even stronger influence on design and engine selection, 192 bhp being required at 32 tonnes. However, with engines available which produced 300 bhp and more this proved no problem for D-B.

Normally, there was power to spare on the less heavy vehicle ranges as well. For example, the L 322 model, a 10.5-tonnes gvw vehicle, had a new power unit fitted in 1961, the OM 322 engine producing 126 bhp; this output represented a power-to-weight ratio of 12 bhp per ton.

The changes in the weight laws coupled with demand for higher payloads within existing gross weight limits resulted in production ceasing on the L 311 and L 312 bonneted models at the end of 1961. These were replaced with semi-forward-control models, the L 323 and L 328, which found particular favour with the construction industry.

Total goods vehicle production in 1962 stood at 44,007 from Daimler-Benz's domestic plants. This figure included 10,140 medium-weights in the 3.6-tonnes to 7-tonnes gross weight categories (some of these were built — up to April 1962 — at Sindelfingen and — from May 1962 — at Duesseldorf). Mannheim (7 tonnes to 14 tonnes gross weight) contributed 21,863 and Gaggenau (12 tonnes to 23 tonnes) 8,019. There was a further 3,985 miscellaneous vehicles produced to make up the final total — which did not include Unimog production of 10,514 vehicles.

In 1962, the Daimler-Benz truck range comprised eight basic models in about 80 standard versions, and the following year saw the introduction of the model identification system that was to be used for Mercedes trucks for the next two decades. All truck models retained the use of the letter L to

The semi-forward-control design was to prove very popular in the 1960s. The L 710 model shown here was built over a 10-year period from 1961 to 1970.

signify Lastkraftwagen (goods vehicle) with further letters indicating configuration — P, for example, indicating Pullman (forward control) and S meaning Sattelzugmaschine (tractor unit). The numbers after the letters then indicated gross weight and engine power output of the engine installed. Thus the LP 608 launched at the Brussels Show in January 1965 reflected that it was a forward-control 6-tonnes gvw truck with an engine producing 80 horsepower. In the same way the designation LP 1620 indicated a forward-control 16-tonner fitted with an engine producing 200 bhp.

The LP/LPS 1620 range and the LP/LPS 1920 replaced the former LP/LPS models and they had a totally new cab. Although this was of a fixed, as opposed to tilting, type it had many of the features which marked it out as ahead of its time. Later, in 1969, heavily updated and made into a tilting unit, it was destined again to be a design in advance of many competitors.

In the early-1960s the new legal requirements, along with

changes in the market, led to development taking place in every sector of major component production. Early in 1964, this was reflected in the announcement of a major change affecting all its diesel engines. The company switched from the pre-combustion chamber indirect-injection ignition concept to direct injection. The first evidence of this was at the Amsterdam Show in February 1964, where D-B unveiled the OM 352 and OM 346. These six-cylinder units, rated for 140 bhp at 2,800 rpm and 220 bhp at 2,200 rpm, respectively, replaced the OM 322 and OM 326.

A new direct-injection engine was also a feature of a new 3-tonner launched at the Brussels Show in January 1965. This was the LP 608, brief mention of which has already been made in reference to the nomenclature system used.

Suitable for payloads of approximately 3 tonnes, the LP 608 had a gross rating of just under 6 tonnes. It offered the choice of three wheelbases — 3.2 m, 3.6 m and 3.8 m — which were suitable for standard body lengths of 3.8 m, 4.5 m and 5.5 m, respectively.

The engine, which had a gross rating of 88 bhp and a cubic capacity of 3.78 litres, was positioned behind the front axle and was matched with a four-speed, all-synchromesh gearbox. Small wheels meant the fitment of 7.00—16 radial-ply tyres, whilst the hydraulic brakes were boosted by air pressure.

A main feature of the LP 608 was the introduction of a new cab, which was effectively a scaled-down version of that fitted on the LP 1620 heavy-duty truck. It had two seats, with the engine housing between them so as to leave the floor area completely flat.

Although the establishment of Woerth was to mean the switch of medium-weight and heavy vehicle production there from Gaggenau and Mannheim, the Gaggenau factory was still producing the ultra-heavies in 1955 when Germany announced the raising of its weight levels for articulated vehicles and lorries and trailers from 32 to 38 tonnes.

The Mercedes-Benz L 319, which was offered with either a 68-bhp petrol engine or a 50-bhp diesel, took Daimler-Benz through the early-1960s in the light van class.

An LP 911 of 1963 being used for street lighting maintenance. It was in 1963 that D-B first started to use this form of designation, LP signifying a forward-control truck and 911 a 9-tonnes payload and a 110-bhp engine.

The cab design on this LPS 1620 tractor unit was introduced in 1963, the vehicle forming just one of an 80-model range offered at that time by the company. It was fitted with a 202-bhp diesel engine — the OM 346.

The Mercedes-Benz OM 346 diesel engine was fitted in many different models in the early-1960s and had a number of ratings. Installed here in an L 1418 semi-forward-control 14-tonner, it was rated at 180 bhp (DIN), or 200 bhp (SAE).

In 1964 Daimler-Benz introduced this LAK 2220 heavy-duty tipper. It was a 6 × 6 outfit built for operation at 22 tonnes gross vehicle weight, the engine fitted producing 200 bhp.

Produced as part of its middleweight forward-control truck programme of the mid-1960s, the company offered this Mercedes-Benz LP 1013 delivery vehicle with a 130-bhp engine for operation at 10 tonnes gross vehicle weight.

Introduced in 1965 as the LB 1513, this chassis was purpose-designed for carrying concrete mixers.

As a result of this legal change, 24-tonne payloads became a practical proposition with appropriately designed articulated outfits. In contrast, the total feasible payload attainable with a lorry and trailer was only 23 tonnes.

Consequently, the 38-tonne artic became attractive to the operator and, from this point on, use of lorry and drawbar trailers in Germany declined in favour of artics. However, there were snags. These arose from the fact that when the law was changed, the permissible axle loading remained at 10 tonnes, whilst a regulation included in German legislation

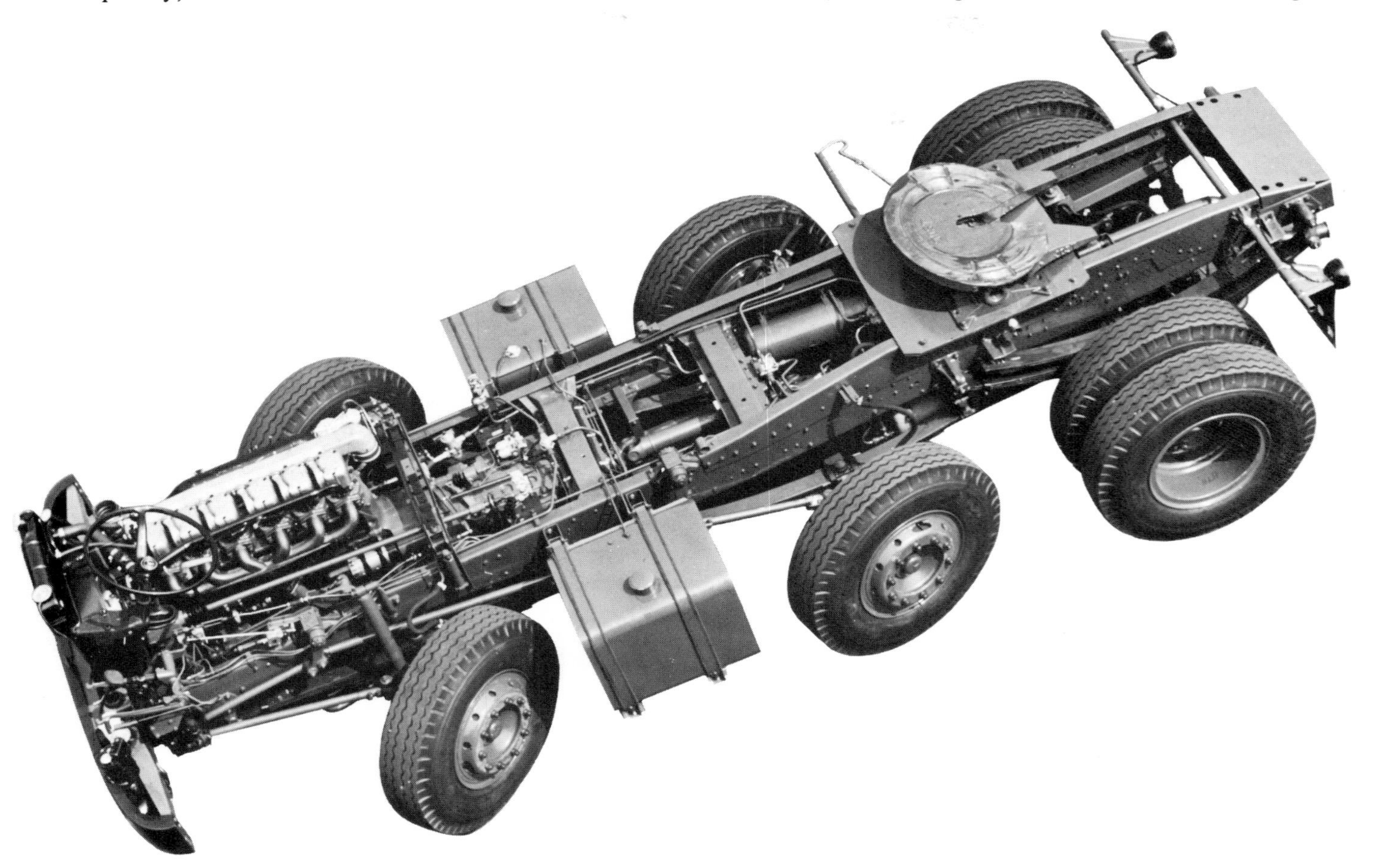

Introduced at the Frankfurt Show of 1965, the LPS 2020 tractor unit (the chassis of which is shown here) was a twin-steer three-axled version of the Mercedes 1620/1920 tractor unit. It was powered by the OM 346 10.8-litre six-cylinder engine rated at 218 bhp.

The LPS 2020 tractor unit, seen here hauling a tank semi-trailer, was perhaps the most successful Mercedes-Benz vehicle of the 1960s. Built for operation at 38 tonnes gcw, the tractor was ahead of its time in terms of cab comfort and driving qualities.

governing turning path and maximum allowable cut-in also remained unchanged at 12 m outer radius and 6.5 m inner radius.

To meet these requirements, taking advantage of the 38-tonnes gcw weight law and obtaining the maximum 12 m body length allowed meant coupling a three-axled tractor unit to a rear-steered semi-trailer with two axles, or using a two-axled tractor with a tri-axled semi-trailer, again with rear steering. A two-axled tractor unit with a two-axled semi-trailer could operate at no more than 36 tonnes without contravening the regulations.

Daimler-Benz was the first German company to produce a tractor unit to meet the new requirements. This was the 6 × 2 LPS 2020, a twin-steer tractor unit which appeared at the Frankfurt Show in 1965 coupled to a Schenk air-sprung semi-trailer fitted with a steering axle. The LPS 2020 was really a three-axle version of the existing 1620/1920 tractor units which had been the main Mercedes tractor unit designs since the weight limit had gone to 32 tonnes. Powered by the OM 346 10.8-litre direct-injection six-cylinder diesel, with an output of 218 bhp at 2,200 rpm, the 2020 had a ZF six-speed constant-mesh gearbox as standard with an 11-speed version

The trend in Germany to high engine power outputs to meet power/weight legal requirements was reflected even in the lighter vehicles. This LP 810, built for operation at 8 tonnes gross, had a 100-bhp (DIN) engine — 110 bhp on the SAE scale — to give it a power/weight ratio of 12.5 bhp per tonne.

of the same box as an option.

Dual-circuit air-brakes and an air-assisted handbrake were standard with a load-sensitive brake valve on the driving axle cutting out the second axle's brakes when running light.

This first offering at 38 tonnes came from the Gaggenau factory, as did two other models to appear at the 1965 Frankfurt Show. These were the LP and LPS 1418 models, available as a two-axled truck at 14.5 tonnes and as a tractor unit for artic operation. Like the 2020, these had the OM 346 engine, but in the 1418 models this was derated to 180 and 200 bhp. When the 2020 was updated for the Frankfurt Show in 1967 the fact that it was fitted with a newly introduced 230-bhp engine, the OM 355, was reflected in its new designation as the LP 2023.

One impact of Woerth on the Mercedes truck programme was to be seen from this point on. On transfer of chassis production from Gaggenau and Mannheim the number of models available came to 19 basic and 150 variations, and these were constantly being supplemented.

In December 1966, for example, a new 12-tonnes gross model was introduced, the LP 1216, fitted with a more powerful 160-bhp engine than the existing LP 1213 design. It

The interior of the cab of an LP 1624 of 1969. Mercedes-Benz cabs of that time were given substantial improvements to enhance the working conditions of the driver.

was designed for drawbar operation at 26.5 tonnes gross train weight. This reflected a move by the German industry towards the fitment of yet more powerful engines.

This power-to-weight increase applied to smaller vehicles just as much as larger ones. Thus, early in 1967, the LP 911, operating at 9 tonnes gross, was fitted with an engine producing 110 bhp, 10 per cent more than the existing LP 910 model.

Nowhere was this move to high-output engines more apparent, of course, than in the heavyweight categories. The move to 38-tonne artics coupled with the 6-bhp-per-tonne power-to-weight ratio requirement generated a need for engines to meet higher engine power outputs than hitherto, 228 bhp being the minimum power requirement at 38 tonnes. Talk of even higher power-to-weight ratios stimulated engine design and Daimler-Benz, along with other German automotive engine manufacturers, stepped up their efforts to produce new families of diesel engines to meet future needs.

Daimler-Benz's 4-tonnes van range had been built for some 10 years when, at the Brussels Show of 1967, new models were announced. These were the L 406 and L 408 and the 0309D and 0309, the L 406 and the 0309D being diesels and the others petrol-engined. A main difference was the use of a separate chassis-frame assembly, rather than the semi-integral construction hitherto featured, and a new cab.

The range consisted of 3.5-tonne, 4-tonne and 4.6-tonne models, with a choice of two wheelbases of 2.95 m and 3.5 m. There was a choice of high and low-compression engines producing 80 bhp and 68 bhp (nett), respectively, against 55 bhp (nett) of the diesel engine. Any of these engines could be specified in the six chassis and chassis-cab versions in the extensive range of 27 different goods vehicle bodies and 12 bus bodies offered.

At the time of the 1967 Frankfurt Show the German industry was suffering. There was a fairly deep depression in heavy goods vehicle sales and some manufacturers, including Daimler-Benz, were concentrating more on the distribution type of vehicle where the market was more stable. Consequently, Daimler-Benz launched its LP 808 chassis at this time; it appeared as a 7.5-tonnes gcw and as an 8-tonnes gvw vehicle with 4.5-tonne and 5-tonne payloads from a low unladen weight of just under 3 tonnes. It featured the same cab as that fitted on the LP 608 and the same 80-bhp diesel engine.

The Frankfurt Show of that year also saw some changes in the Mercedes ultra-heavy models. There was the 2023 already mentioned, and the engine used in this model, the OM 355, a 11.6-litre longer-stroke version of the established OM 346 design, was also installed in two new tractor units for

Substantial changes to its heavier vehicle models were made by Daimler-Benz in 1968. This is the LPS 2024, a twin-steer 6 × 2, the designation of which indicates a raising of the engine power to 240 bhp (DIN).

Daimler-Benz made a strong bid in the 1960s for the market connected with the building and construction business with vehicles like this LPK 1620, which had two- or, optionally, three-stage suspension, telescopic shock absorbers and torsion-bar stabilizers on the front and rear axles.

38-tonnes gcw operation. Both of these were designated LPS 2223, but one was a 6 × 2 model and the other a 6 × 4. The LP 2223 was also offered as a solo version at 22-tonnes gvw in 6 × 2 and 6 × 4 form.

The outstanding feature of these vehicles was the suspension, with the technical press at the time commenting on the smooth ride and stability it afforded on corners. It comprised 1.8-m long front springs with 1.4-m long units at the rear supplemented by telescopic dampers on each axle and anti-roll bars on the first and third axles.

The impact of the acquisition of Hanomag-Henschel in the spring of 1969 was not immediately apparent to the outside observer. The technical concepts of the Hanomag-Henschel light transporter range were retained until the Mercedes L 206D and L 306D were introduced in 1971, based on the Hanomag F 20 and F 35.

Production of the Henschel medium and heavy-duty designs continued for a while until the rationalization of production referred to in the preceding chapter could be implemented.

Quite apart from the Hanomag-Henschel acquisition, however, 1969 was an important year for Daimler-Benz

The LAS 1920 model of 1965, shown here, had an unusual semi-trailer. The body at the front was a two-way tipper, while that at the rear was a three-way design.

products, and the Frankfurt Show of that year provided the opportunity to unveil these. It was very much an engine show, not only for Daimler-Benz, but for German manufacturers generally.

This was because the legislators in Germany had indicated that an 8-bhp-per-tonne power-to-weight ratio was coming. This meant that a power output of 304 bhp would be necessary at 38 tonnes. Consequently, engine manufacturers designed new power units with 300 bhp and more as the target.

Daimler-Benz tackled the situation in two ways. Detail changes were made to all the Mercedes direct-injection engines with additional power and a reduction in engine speed as the main aims. This was effected largely through change in the injection pump design and the piston shape.

These modifications, however, were overshadowed by the unveiling of a totally new power unit, the 320-bhp OM 403, a 90-degrees V-10 water-cooled direct-injection engine.

It was the first in a series, being derived from a family of V-8, V-10 and V-12 engines developed by Daimler-Benz as multi-fuel units for military purposes. A feature was its remarkably light weight: at 910 kg it was some 25 per cent lighter than comparable V-8s with similar power outputs.

It had a capacity of 16 litres, with a bore and stroke of 125 mm and 130 mm, respectively. It turned out to be the forerunner of Daimler-Benz's truck engine range of the 1970s, the 400 series, to be produced in co-operation with MAN. This power unit programme covered V-4, V-6, V-8, V-10, V-12 and in-line engines, and it provided for the manufacture of Mercedes and MAN versions.

The Frankfurt Show of 1969 was also notable for Daimler-Benz because it marked the launch of a new forward-control range of articulated tractor units and drawbar trailer-hauling rigid vehicles, designated LP 2232 and LPS 2232; the LP 2232 was a 6 × 4, the LPS 2232 a twin-steering 6 × 2.

These featured the new V-10 engine and the existing cab had been modified and made to tilt hydraulically. This was available as a day cab, with two-bunk sleeper facility, and also as a full sleeper.

Other introductions for these vehicles were an air-assisted clutch and all-synchromesh gearbox. The single-dry-plate 420-mm diameter clutch was matched to a new ZF synchromesh gearbox, basically offering four speeds with an additional planetary gear set.

A further noteworthy appearance at the 1969 Frankfurt Show was a complete range of Mercedes vehicles fitting air suspension on all axles. These were introduced as part of a broad plan of Daimler-Benz to offer vehicles purpose-built for particular uses, in this case for handling demountable bodies. This concept was to be taken considerably further in the 1970s, the air-suspension idea being applied to vehicles tailored for the needs of particular trades and industries.

As the 1960s closed, the company's production hit record levels and the total number of commercial vehicles produced in 1970, counting the Hanomag-Henschel contribution, was 171,362, compared with 146,104 in 1969. Yet further expansion was to come in the next decade as Daimler-Benz consolidated its position in international markets.

Chapter 5

The 1970s: More power and refinement

Brief reference was made in the last chapter to the use of air suspension on selected Mercedes models, particularly for lift-on, lift-off body use, where the suspension system was used to raise and lower the body. Transport users in Germany were among the first to adopt demountable body systems. The swop-body concept was, however, but one part of a strong drive in Germany to match body types and dimensions to the needs of production and distribution processes.

Daimler-Benz took the lead in this, tying up with several German bodybuilders to produce systems for certain industries. Take the food trade, for example. Here, one of the main bodybuilders, Blumhardt, of Wuppertal, had a body concept — called the Rationorm system — which was tailored largely for producer-to-wholesaler and wholesaler-to-supermarket operation.

Three types of vehicles were evolved for trunk-haulage duties — all drawbar trailer outfits employing the LP and LPS 1519/48 and LP and LPS 1519/51 Mercedes chassis. The LP 1519/51 was fitted with the 192-bhp Mercedes engine and was for operation at up to 30.8 tonnes gross train weight.

Four rigid box van vehicles were available for food distribution purposes. The smallest was an 11-tonner and this was followed by two types of 13-tonner and four types of 14/15-tonne vehicle. There were big differences among the 14/15 tonners — two of these were low-powered and two were high-powered versions. The idea was to offer vehicles for both light but bulky loads and relatively bulky but heavy products.

As an alternative, or in addition to the use of drawbar trailers and rigid vehicles, two types of articulated vehicle were offered as part of the system and there were five variations on these two basic designs. The smallest artic here was the Mercedes LPS 1313, fitted with a 168-bhp engine and designed for operation at 21 tonnes. This power level was significant because an 8-bhp-per-tonne ratio came into force on January 1, 1971, in the first instance for all vehicles up to 28.5 tonnes gross weight. Its application to heavier vehicles came later.

In contrast with the four other versions of the articulated outfit — all Mercedes LPS 1319 vehicles — 192-bhp engines were fitted. The two lightest versions of these were built for operating at 23 tonnes, so they had to satisfy the 8-bhp requirement. In contrast, the other two were built for operation at 29 tonnes and so could only be placed on the road until December 31, 1971. After that they had to be fitted with engines of greater power output.

This concept of tailoring models for particular industries extended to the construction industry, furniture transport and refrigerated vehicle movements and was an important influence on vehicle design.

The early-1970s saw the steady integration of the Hanomag-Henschel models. In 1971, the Mercedes 55-bhp car engine was introduced in the Mercedes L 206D and L 306D light-transporter models and in the following year the

As the 1960s moved into the 1970s Daimler-Benz produced a number of vehicle ranges tailored to the needs of specific trades and industries. This LPS 1319 artic was designed with bodywork purpose-built for use in supplying supermarkets.

A vehicle purpose-developed for supermarket deliveries, and fitted with a tail-lift for handling wheeled stillages, seen unloading at a small branch of a leading German supermarket chain.

One of the last hybrids (an LAPK 1632) to be produced after the acquisition of Henschel in that it features the Hanomag-Henschel cab, but incorporates Mercedes-Benz components including the 320-bhp V-10 engine. Kassel-built LK and LAK 2624s were supplied for export during the 1970s due to insufficient capacity at Woerth.

Mercedes 1.8-litre petrol engine was added as a further option.

Commenting at the time, Daimler-Benz said: 'They are based on the technical concept of the Hanomag-Henschel transporter models F 20 through F 35, but do have a considerable number of different versions and equipment modifications.'

The company went on to say that the Hanomag-Henschel production programme had been augmented by the addition of the 'box' types of the Duesseldorf transporter programme and the inclusion of Mercedes-Benz chassis of the 13 and 15-tonne classes.

Although there were these changes, the main step towards a Mercedes, as opposed to a Hanomag-Henschel light van range occurred at the Brussels Show in 1973. Already the success of its move into this 2 to 4-tonnes class could be measured. More than 250 different versions were offered and production and sales of light transporters in 1972 was up by 28,000 on 1968 sales levels (the last full year of Hanomag-Henschel production). The Brussels Show models of 1973, however, reflected many new developments. The whole braking system, for example, was revised, a dual-circuit braking system being introduced along with an increase in braking area and better cooling of the brake drums. There were also further modifications to the cab to afford greater safety and comfort for the driver.

A heavy-duty 6 × 6 truck powered by the Mercedes-Benz V-10 engine in 355-bhp form on test in Germany with tipper bodywork installed.

The OM 401 V-6 engine (upper left) introduced in 1972 formed the smallest of the revolutionary engine range introduced at this time. Other engines in the series included the OM 402 V-8 (upper right), the OM 403 V-10 (lower left) and the OM 404 V-12 (lower right).

There were in-line engines in the engine range introduced in 1972 which owed a great deal to the V-engine developments. This is the OM 407 six-cylinder unit.

An early application of the OM 401 V-6 engine showing the gearchange linkage above the engine, enabling the cab to be sealed against heat and noise.

The introduction of a new rear axle with increased axle loads brought about changes in the running gear. The tubular frame was retained, but it was considerably broadened at the rear axle and equipped with a leaf-spring suspension. The tube-type axle introduced had leaf springs and was equipped with two diagonal telescopic shock absorbers. The new broadened frame offered room for a 60-litre fuel tank.

As an alternative to the 2.2-litre diesel engine with 60 bhp (DIN), the more powerful 70-bhp (DIN) petrol engine was offered as an option.

The heavier vehicles of the Henschel range were given considerable attention with Mercedes main components being introduced as a first stage to complete integration. For example, two heavy-construction 6 × 6 vehicles designated LAPK 1632 and LAPK 2632, fitted with the 320-bhp OM 403 V-10 engine and the Hanomag-Henschel cab but badged

Introduced at the Frankfurt Show of 1979, the OM 422 LA V-8 engine was boosted by turbocharging to 375 bhp (DIN). The turbocharger is shown at the rear of the right-hand cylinder bank.

Described as a key feature of Daimler-Benz's flagship for the 1980s, this updated version of the New Generation cab was introduced in 1979. Another feature of the vehicle was the OM 422 LA turbocharged engine installed at this time. It was rated to produce 375 bhp at 2,300 rpm.

Mercedes, were produced during a relatively short period from 1972 to 1973.

The LAPK 1632, with a gross vehicle weight of 16 tonnes, and the LAPK 2632/6 × 6, with a gross vehicle weight of either 22 or 26 tonnes, were designed for operation with a trailer at 38 tonnes gcw.

When the German industry moved into the 1970s the main preoccupation was with high engine power outputs. January 1, 1971 was selected as the operative date for the introduction of the 8-bhp-per-tonne ratio for vehicles and combinations of up to 28.5 tonnes gross weight. A further 12 months was given for vehicles of over this weight to meet the requirement.

Daimler-Benz was not very happy about the development.

Powered by a 375-bhp turbocharged diesel engine, this heavy-duty combination comprising a 4 × 2 tractor unit and a three-axled semi-trailer is scheduled for long-distance haulage duties and features improved cab comfort including additional sound insulation material to improve the driver's environment.

Pursuing its policy of offering vehicles to suit national market requirements, this Bremen van was made available on the French market with the Mercedes-Benz 2.4-litre diesel engine and automatic transmission.

A low-angle view of the 407D transporter showing clearly the leaf springs and telescopic shock absorbers of the front suspension. Customers requiring a more powerful version of this vehicle could specify the 409D, powered by a five-cylinder diesel developing 88 bhp, in place of the 72 bhp of the four-cylinder unit fitted to this model.

In the 1972 annual report the company commented: 'Because of this minimum-horsepower law, which applies only in the Federal Republic, the ability of German transport firms to compete beyond our national borders has been seriously impaired. In order to eliminate this competitive distortion in the newly expanded Common Market, it is essential that the laws concerning vehicle weights, dimensions and minimum performance be harmonized.'

Daimler-Benz nevertheless was prepared for the situation with its 400-series diesel family which, with V-6, V-8 and V-12 versions produced to supplement the V-10, covered a power spread from 130 to 430 bhp on the DIN scale in naturally-aspirated form. When turbocharged, the range could be extended to offer outputs of up to 570 bhp.

The naturally-aspirated V-6 was offered initially with a power output of 192 bhp, the V-8 256 bhp, the V-10 320 bhp and the V-12 430 bhp. In turbocharged form the rating of

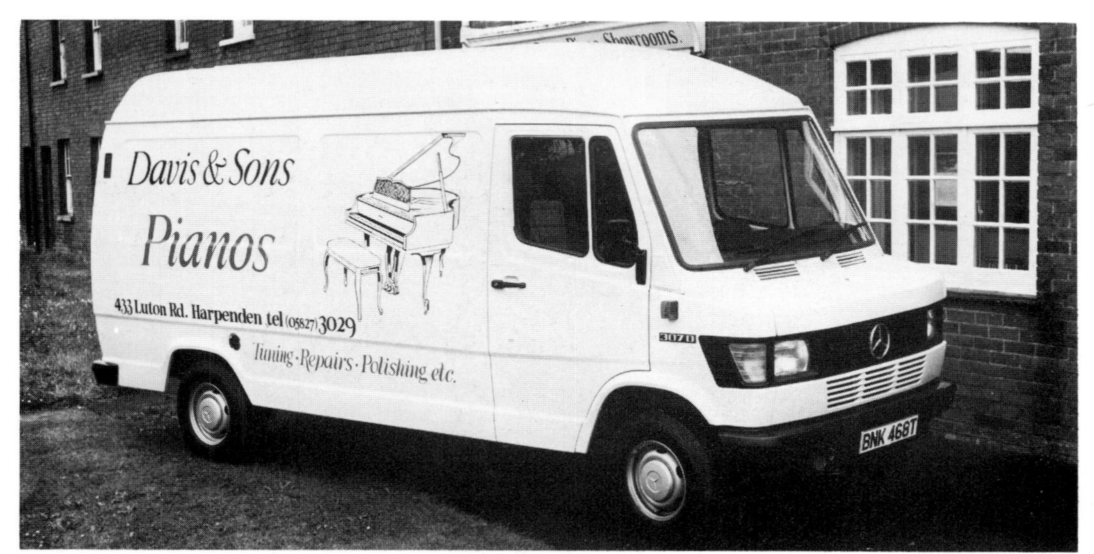

Unusual duty for a 307D with high-roof van body. To facilitate the loading and unloading of the heavy instruments this vehicle was equipped with a tail-lift similar to those used frequently on ambulances and welfare vehicles.

A three-axled 2032S 6 × 2 tractor unit with sleeper cab built for international operations and seen here coupled to a Blumhardt refrigerated semi-trailer.

The favourable fuel economy of this Mercedes-Benz 1619 S tractor unit, seen here coupled to a refrigerated semi-trailer, was a major factor in its choice by the British Beef Company for its haulage fleet.

these engines were 255 bhp for the V-6, 340 bhp for the V-8, 425 bhp for the V-10 and 570 bhp for the V-12.

The 400 series did not only comprise vee-engines. There was an in-line four-cylinder producing 130 bhp, a five-cylinder producing 160 bhp and an in-line six producing 192 bhp. There were also a longer-stroke in-line five and an in-line six producing 192 bhp and 225 bhp, respectively.

Although the bore at 125 mm was common to all these engines, there was a variation in the stroke which ranged from 130 mm through 140 mm to 150 mm according to the engine. However, it was emphasized at the time that it was quite possible that not all these engines, although fully developed, would go into series production.

There was, as indicated in the last chapter, a joint production agreement with MAN covering certain aspects of these engines. There was in addition an agreement with the same company for the development of planetary gear hub-reduction axles. These were fitted on a new range of on-and-off-highway tippers in the 16-tonnes to 26-tonnes gross weight bracket, as was the 400-series engine. Available in forward-control and bonneted form, the range comprised 19 models, with or without all-wheel drive and including both two and three-axle versions. The engines offered in these machines were the OM 401 V-6 developing 192 bhp, the OM 402 V-8 and the OM 403 V-10.

All these vehicles had ZF transmissions; the S6-80 and the S6-90 six-speed synchromesh gearboxes with splitter boxes available as options on the six and eight-cylinder engines,

Elegant styling was a feature of the Duesseldorf van range. Here are two examples of the L 608D diesel-engined version of 1979. Roller-shutter doors on each side of the long-wheelbase body are a feature of the milk-delivery vehicle below.

An interesting open-sided body on the 16-tonne 1617 chassis, which was chosen by Shippams for the distribution of their food pastes from warehouse to city-centre shops.

Three models at 10 tonnes, 12 tonnes and 14 tonnes gvw were offered in the New Generation middleweight range. A power output from 130 bhp (DIN) to 240 bhp (DIN) was offered from the engines fitted in these models.

with the nine-speed range change 5S-110GP for the V-10.

Perhaps the most important feature of these new models, however, was the cab, for this gave Mercedes medium and heavyweight vehicles a totally different identity. A great deal of attention was paid in the new cab to driver comfort. It featured a new system of cab suspension to isolate the driver from the effects of poor road surfaces. This utilized pivoting bearings with elastic rubber bushes in front and coil springs and shock absorbers at the rear of the cab. The system, combined with the vehicle's long leaf springs and powerful shock absorbers, was designed to give optimum driving comfort.

In designing the cab, attention was given to achieving a low air-resistance and a non-aggressive appearance, whilst aerodynamic styling to reduce soiling of side windows by road dirt was a feature. Easily read instruments, powerful heating and ventilation and an anatomically correct driving seat also made their contribution to increased driver comfort.

An extremely rigid cab construction, with the interior reinforced by large pressed-steel parts and the front panel featuring a double shell, was aimed to provide a high degree of passive safety. The dashboard was covered by foam safety padding, as were the doors, roof frame supports and rear wall.

The fitment of the 400 series engines in the Mercedes tipper/dump truck range occurred in time for the Frankfurt Show of 1973, and it was the prelude to much bigger things for it was followed in the summer of 1974 by the introduction of an all-embracing new range of heavies for operation at up to 40 tonnes gross combination weight, which came to be known as the Mercedes 'New Generation' range, designed around the unitary component principle, which permitted rationalization of both production methods and components.

The features of the forward-control tippers, including the cab, were carried into the general haulage models except that a two-bunk sleeper version of the cab was added.

From that point on the New Generation range was steadily expanded and the Brussels Show, in January 1975, saw the introduction of the first New Generation 16-tonne rigid, the 1619, for solo operation. This had the 192-bhp OM 401 V-6

There were three different versions offered of the New Generation Mercedes cab: a day cab for short-distance work, a more comfortable long-haul version and a sleeper for international haulage.

Daimler-Benz decided to offer an air-spoiler for cab-mounting on the New Generation cab where the vehicle was used with a high body; fitment could mean fuel savings of up to 10 per cent.

engine.

Then, at Frankfurt in the same year, the range was extended further downward with a medium-weight class consisting of 10, 12 and 14-tonners. These reflected a widening of the 400 series engine production, for the new models fitted, respectively, the straight six-cylinder OM 352 producing 130 bhp, the turbocharged OM 352A producing 168 bhp and the V-6 OM 401 producing 192 bhp. In addition, there was a new 14-tonne tractor unit, the 1424S, fitted with the V-8 OM 402 engine derated to develop 240 bhp.

Mercedes-Benz gearboxes were fitted on all these new models — a five-speed unit on the 10-tonner and eight or nine-speed units on the 12- and 14-tonners.

That Frankfurt Show also saw the New Generation treatment being applied to one of the company's most successful — but 10 years old in design — models, the 2032S. This included the fitting of a special double frame, so avoiding the necessity for a subframe, as well as more precise steering and a rearrangement of axle positions.

Four weight classes (2.55, 2.8, 3.2 and 3.5 tonnes) were offered in the Bremen light van range, along with two wheelbase lengths and two different roof versions. The vehicle shown here is the 307D diesel, short-wheelbase, high-roof model.

Apart from the mediumweight introductions of 1975, there were a number of developments in the lighter vehicle sectors. Daimler-Benz announced more powerful diesel and petrol engines for its medium-size Transporter models and a longer body for the top-weight L 508D and L 608D Transporters. The L 406D and L 408 were supplemented by two new designations, the L 407D and L 409, indicating that they were fitted with more powerful engines broadly similar to those installed in the 240D (diesel) and 230P (petrol) passenger cars.

The L 407D was powered by the OM 616 four-cylinder overhead-camshaft diesel engine developing 65 bhp at 4,300 rpm.

The M 115 four-cylinder ohc petrol engine of the L 409 was designed to run on regular-grade fuel. It was of 2,307-cc capacity and developed 90 bhp at 4,800 rpm.

There was yet another development at the 1975 Frankfurt Show. This was in the field of automatic transmissions and it had three features — the announcement of a four-speed automatic transmission (the W4A 018) for Transporter models; the unveiling of a prototype automatic transmission (the W4B 035) for lightweight trucks up to 9 tonnes gvw; and a four-speed automatic transmission (the W4B 080) with hydraulic retarder for heavy-duty trucks applications.

One of the first stages in the welding of the Hanomag-Henschel light vans into the Daimler-Benz set-up was the installation of this Mercedes-Benz 2.2-litre, 60-bhp (DIN) engine in what became the Mercedes-Benz L206/306D range.

The company said at the time that these transmissions had been introduced to meet the needs of short-range vehicles, notably transporters, refuse collectors and distribution vehicles.

Interest then moved on to light vans as the company in the Spring of 1977 introduced a new van range in the 1-tonne to 2-tonne payload class — the Bremen range.

This was a completely new design, offered in a wide variety of wheelbases and as a van, pickup truck, combi and minibus. The power units offered were the Mercedes 65-bhp diesel and the 85-bhp petrol engine as an alternative. Such was the success of the new range that the company was able in its 1977 annual report to indicate that 40,257 Bremen vans of up to 4 tonnes gvw were built, the previous year's production almost

A further part of putting the Mercedes stamp on the Hanomag-Henschel light van was the introduction of Mercedes-Benz seating and steering in the existing cab.

The front-wheel-drive Hanomag-Henschel light van could be operated as a six-wheeler. This is one of the first examples to be badged as a Mercedes after Daimler-Benz had acquired the Hanomag concern.

The OM 352 Mercedes-Benz six-cylinder diesel engine, first offered with a power output range from 65 to 90 bhp (DIN), later had a 130-bhp version added, all for fitment in the Duesseldorf van range.

being equalled in spite of the model changeover.

This initial success was to be built upon, total production topping 100,000 by the Frankfurt Show in 1979, when power-assisted steering and automatic transmissions were announced for the diesel-engined versions.

The changes made to the Bremen range had been preceded earlier in the year by Duesseldorf van changes. At the Turin Motor Show in the May of 1979 new versions were announced to meet the need for a van with a particularly large and wide loading area. They fitted newly developed axle units with a wider track previously used on the bus version of Mercedes model O 309. This standard-production box van thus had a loading width and load area previously found only with special bodies. The sliding side door had an interior width of 1,100 mm so that goods could be loaded on pallets.

The following four versions were made available: L 508D,

Basically the Hanomag-Henschel light transporter design, this 306D tipper vehicle was badged as a Mercedes-Benz after the takeover.

By adding a trailer axle to this LP 813 model, Daimler-Benz evolved this vehicle in 1979 for demountable body hauling at 16 tonnes gross weight.

2,080 kg payload and 5,190 kg gross weight; L 608D, 2,365 kg payload and 5,600 kg gross weight; L 608D, 3,225 kg payload and 6,790 kg gross weight; and L 613D, 3,150 kg payload and 6,790 kg gross weight.

The L 508D/L 608D used the four-cylinder direct-injection OM 314 engine, which has an output of 85 bhp (DIN), and the L 613D used the six-cylinder OM 352 engine, with an output of 130 bhp.

The main announcement at Frankfurt in 1979, however, was of a twin turbocharged V-8 engine. A development of the

Inside the Mercedes-Benz cab for the 1980s. Note the window area, the instrument grouping, the centre tray for documents and other refinements.

The type 2032 S tractor unit in 6 × 2 and 6 × 4 form, built for operation at 38 tonnes gross combination weight, was introduced in this form with the New Generation cab at the Frankfurt Show of 1975.

A Bremen-built van of 1977; this one was delivered for operation in Britain. Note the excellent visibility afforded by the deep windscreen and sloping-edge cab door windows.

company's 400-series engine and designated the OM 422LA, the turbocharged, after-cooled power unit produced 375 bhp at 2,300 rpm and delivered a maximum torque of 1,143 lb ft at 1,200 rpm.

This turbocharged unit was the big brother of another new engine, the naturally-aspirated OM 422, producing 280 bhp at 2,300 rpm and a maximum torque of 767 lb ft at 1,200 rpm.

A little later, the OM 427A followed, the turbocharged versions producing 350 bhp at 2,300 rpm and a maximum torque of 1,039 lb ft at 1,200 rpm. These engines had a larger cubic capacity than the existing V-8 engine, at 14.62 litres, which had been obtained by increasing both bore and stroke dimensions. Their high-torque low-revving characteristics were in line with the general trend towards 'economy' engines, and they had exceptionally good specific fuel consumption figures. They were built at Mannheim alongside

Two popular Mercedes-Benz mediumweights of the late-1970s: the LP 709 (left) built primarily for local delivery work and the 1013 (right) for both local and medium-distance operation.

Box vans (high top and conventional), a crew-bus and a drop-side truck from the Bremen range. Those shown here were equipped with the four-cylinder OM 616 diesel engine developing 65 bhp.

A Duesseldorf L 608D 7.5-tonne box van being used in Britain on long-distance operation between England and Scotland and equipped with an 80-bhp diesel engine and five-speed gearbox.

This handsome Mercedes-Benz 1626 S tractor unit, hauling a York box-van semi-trailer, was purchased specifically for international haulage between Britain, Holland, Belgium and Germany by GAF (Great Britain). Note the clever use of the cab roof spoiler by the operator for publicity purposes.

the existing OM 402 256-bhp V-8 range.

To permit the fitment of the new turbocharged engines, both the front end of the chassis and the New Generation heavy truck cab were modified, this version being called the G cab. Its development stemmed largely from the need to increase cooling capacity, although the twin turbochargers obviously added to the bulk. The G cab was, in fact, 160 mm wider and 80 mm higher externally. There were detail changes to the interior and improvements in the in-cab noise levels.

Power train arrangements for the new engines saw interesting innovations. Eaton constant-mesh gearboxes were offered for the first time as a manufacturer's option by Mercedes, as alternatives to ZF synchromesh units.

New ZF gearboxes with 16 speeds and rear axles with lower ratios were introduced to optimize fuel consumption and match the performance of the new engines.

Chapter 6

Purpose-building for world markets

As an exporter of commercial vehicles, Daimler-Benz holds the unique record of selling the first trucks it ever built outside its own country; they went to the USA and Britain. Even when commercial vehicles were first accepted — reluctantly — in Germany the main customers were to be found outside, mainly in Europe and including Russia.

That was in the late-1890s and early-1900s. Later, they found their way to all parts of the world, initially in completely built-up form and later as knocked-down and sub-assembled units. But the real success of the company has come in the last 30 years!

In the period immediately after the Second World War, 1948 stands out as the year in which Daimler-Benz finished consolidating in order to move forward. This applied just as much in export markets as in Germany. There were then just four Daimler-Benz companies outside the Federal Republic. These were in Vienna, Zurich, Budapest and London and they were concerned with private cars rather than commercial vehicles. The postwar export effort, which also dates from that time, concentrated initially on cars rather than trucks or buses, the 1949 figures revealing a very modest DM 6m exports in that year. But the Daimler-Benz export staff were not slow to exploit chances, for 1950 saw a massive increase to DM 66m, exports going to over 50 countries in Europe and overseas, and to DM 156m in 1951 to 65 countries.

In these years, the export emphasis was on completely built-up units, a situation which shortly was to change to some degree with the establishment of assembly and manufacturing facilities at Buenos Aires, in the Argentine, and Sao Paulo, in Brazil.

One of the most significant moves at this time involved negotiations with Tata Locomotive Engineering Company of Bombay. As a result, in March 1953, the Indian and German companies entered into a 15-year technical aid agreement for Tata to assemble and manufacture Mercedes trucks for the Indian market at its factory at Jamshedpur.

The following year saw three type 300 Mercedes 4½-tonners running successfully in a rally from Germany to Bombay and back, an extremely arduous overland trip which involved travelling over 13,000 km in widely varying road conditions. This proved very useful to the company in revealing design weaknesses, which could be corrected in the early stages of manufacture of the Indian product.

Progress in India was immediate. The planned production of 3,000 trucks a year was reached in the first year and the target build was set at 6,000 from 1956 onwards. There was a massive injection of capital as a result of funding in association with Indian banks, and yet further expansion raised production to an annual level of 12,000 vehicles in 1961.

Such was the programme in India that Daimler-Benz in its 1961 report indicated that, from the start of production in 1953, over 53,000 Tata-Mercedes trucks had been built at the Jamshedpur works. With the production rate running at

The Mercedes-Benz do Brasil factory at Sao Paulo from the air.

1,000 a month it was then planned to increase the plant's capacity to double annual production to 24,000 a year by 1966.

In South America, meanwhile, an Argentinian company had been set up — Mercedes-Benz Argentina SA of Buenos Aires. This built both private cars and light diesel trucks and in the 1950s it expanded and consolidated its position. By the start of the 1960s it was producing the main truck model built — the L312 — at the rate of 300 a month. The economic climate in South America was uncertain, however, and 1962 saw a big drop in truck production to 2,516 from the 1961 total of 3,568, with a further fall to 1,550 in 1963.

In Brazil, what was subsequently to be the biggest truck plant in South America was constructed at Sao Bernardo do Campo in the early-1950s. Political instability following the death of the Brazilian president of that time restricted development, however, before the operation truly got into its stride. Even then, there were fluctuations in production because of the country's unsettled economic state. By way of example, 1961 saw a production drop of 26 per cent to 6,999 trucks from the 1960 total. Yet the following year it was back to 8,937 before falling even more steeply to 5,700 in 1963.

Apart from the establishment of its overseas factories, the company also stepped up its direct exports of completely built-up and kit chassis from its domestic factories. The emphasis was on bonneted units at this time, as it was for its

The truck assembly line at the Sao Paulo factory of Mercedes-Benz do Brasil

own domestic market in Germany.

Kit export, even in the 1980s, plays a major part in Daimler-Benz's role as an exporter so it is appropriate, perhaps, at this stage to look at this part of Daimler-Benz's history, concentrating on the boom period — the last 30 years.

It was at the beginning of the 1950s that ckd consignments

Cabs moving steadily along for fitting to trucks being built at the Daimler-Benz factory in Brazil.

started to flow in quantity from the Daimler-Benz works in Germany to its foreign subsidiaries and overseas assemblers.

The company explains that many buyer countries wished to build up their own industries. The developing countries in particular regarded their own commercial vehicle assembly as a chance to train specialists and to provide new jobs.

A high proportion of all vehicle types from the Woerth works — light, mediumweight and heavy trucks — are sent ckd to some 20 countries in Europe, Africa, Asia, Australia and South America. They make up almost one-third of the daily production volume of this factory.

In some countries, however, permission to establish assembly plants was only given on condition that the local content should be increased continuously. As a result, three main types of export consignment have been developed by Daimler-Benz.

There is the standard consignment, which includes all parts of the vehicle as they enter the assembly line in the main works in Woerth. A second standard consignment is virtually the same, but with a cab in the form of separate, unpainted sheet-metal parts and a knocked-down frame. Finally, there is the special assortment of parts as residual consignment to companies with an extensive local content.

About 80 per cent of the total volume of ckd consignments from Woerth belong to the second group. Daimler-Benz points out that, as a matter of course, certain parts produced by the subsidiary, or purchased from suppliers in the importing country, are subject to Daimler-Benz approval. This is quite easy, the company says, with parts like rear-view mirrors or rubber strips, but the better the quality or operating safety required of the component, the more thorough the procedure. Samples have to be sent in, design drawings scrutinized carefully, materials' specifications adhered to and the prospective suppliers' product subjected to the same stringent quality controls as are carried out in the German works.

The export programme includes an approximate total of 330 model versions, from light goods vehicles to heavy six-wheel trucks, standard or all-wheel drive, bonneted and forward-control cabs, artic tractor units and bus chassis. As a considerable proportion of ckd consignments are exported to

An 11-tonne gross Mercedes-Benz box van from the company's Brazilian factory photographed in Sao Paulo in 1978.

A Brazilian-built LS 1924 40-tonne artic seen operating in Southern Brazil towards the end of the 1970s.

regions with a British background, about 60 per cent are right-hand-drive versions.

Daimler-Benz explains that once an assembly project has been passed, the Production Planning Department (Foreign Countries) takes charge. Complicated assembly equipment is usually delivered by the parent company, which subjects it to practical tests before it is exported. Daimler-Benz assembly advisors supervise the setting up and the initial phase of production. It is through these assembly advisors, who are expected to be not only experienced technicians and instructors but also, quite often, adroit tacticians and skilful negotiators, that the contact with the parent company is established and maintained.

Back, then, to the build-up of foreign subsidiaries and assembly plants where there was a flurry of expansion in the late-1960s. It is appropriate to pick out the commercial vehicle highlights.

In India, production levels at Tata Engineering reached 20,641 in 1968. Daimler-Benz's successful agreement was, however, drawing to a close. It expired on March 31, 1969,

CKD kits are packed together in ISO freight containers for despatch overseas at Daimler-Benz's factory at Woerth.

The engine factory of the Iranian Diesel Engine Manufacturing Company at Tabriz, in Iran, assembles Mercedes-Benz diesel engines for installation in trucks and buses.

and was replaced by a limited licence agreement, as the Indian authorities required changes. Daimler-Benz, however, continued to hold 11.5 per cent of the company's equity. Tata has gone from strength to strength since that time, with D-B increasing its financial interest to 12.7 per cent in 1979.

With the acquisition of Hanomag-Henschel in the 1960s, Daimler-Benz also acquired a substantial interest (25.5 per cent) in another Indian company, Bajaj Tempo Ltd, of Poona, which for many years successfully built the Hanomag light van range for the Indian market.

In South America in the late-1960s expansion was aided by growing stability in Brazil, where government policies were curbing the galloping inflation which hitherto had been a characteristic of the country's economy.

By 1969, Mercedes-Benz do Brasil was reporting an annual production of 17,278 commercial vehicles to give Mercedes a 42 per cent market share. The company there spent DM 45m on expanding and modernizing its manufacturing facilities and its product line. It also bought the largest privately owned foundry in South America to supply castings.

The 1970s saw the whole Daimler-Benz commercial vehicle operation take off in Brazil. Commercial vehicle production there improved from 19,850 in 1971 to 26,272 in 1972, then 32,877 in 1973 and 43,600 in 1974. The upward rise of the sales curve then tended to flatten-off, but the company was building some 60,000 trucks annually as the 1970s closed. Daimler-Benz commented in 1973: 'This continued growth is attributable both to the successful favourable automobile boom in Brazil and to the successful introduction in 1972 of the small truck type L 608D. By the end of 1973 this vehicle achieved a market penetration of approximately 44 per cent.'

In 1974 the company commented: 'With a market penetration of about 45 per cent (3 tonnes gvw and over) and of about 90 per cent for buses, our subsidiary company is by far the greatest supplier of commercial vehicles in the Brazilian market.'

It is interesting to see how once a country gets a firmly based automotive industry, it in turn looks for a strong export market. Such thinking is reflected in this Daimler-Benz comment, also made in 1974: 'In conformity with government-encouraged export efforts for the industry, the company was again able to expand export sales. Important markets are traditionally the South and Central American countries as well as increasingly some of the African countries and the USA.' The comment about the US was shortly to prove of special significance as the Brazilian factory was becoming the springboard for Daimler-Benz's commercial vehicle entry into the US market.

The products of the Brazilian factory were also finding their way elsewhere to places as far away as Turkey, Nigeria and Angola, as well as other South and Central American countries. These activities were sponsored by the Brazilian Government and such were the levels that in 1979 no less than 7,025 vehicles were exported.

Production had reached such a high level at Sao Bernardo do Campo, however, that the company decided to expand it by building a sub-plant for buses at Campinas, some 100 km away from the main plant. This was in production by 1978.

In Argentina, as in Brazil, the 1950s and 1960s were difficult, but 1969 was a record year for Daimler-Benz with production totalling 6,221, representing a 35 per cent market share. It was an important year in another way, too, for the production line of the Buenos Aires factory was extended to build the L 608 and take up the assembly of Unimog vehicles. The boom, however, was to be short-lived.

In Argentina, commercial vehicle sales in 1972, at 8,269, dipped from the 1971 figure of 8,496 and Mercedes-Benz' Argentinian business development 'was negatively affected by the continuing cost increases'. As a result net income 'was affected by the inadequate sales prices and was declining after translation in DM'.

Things were not any better in the following year for the Argentinian company's results were hit by reduced commercial vehicle demand. Sales again fell — to 7,823 — but on the brighter side, exports of these to Andes Pact countries came to 1,600 units.

Difficult economic conditions continued throughout the mid-1970s, which had a depressing affect on the Argentinian company's productivity and profitability. Things did not start to improve until towards the end of the decade; in 1979 sales moved to 9,042 commercial vehicles, partly through a drop in the (galloping) inflation rate and partly through the introduction of new chassis for city buses and heavy-duty trucks.

In the 1960s, Daimler-Benz's top management turned its attention to other markets than India and South America. In the Middle East, Daimler-Benz's activities initially centred on Iran, and in the period from 1965 to 1969 D-B reported that exports to that country doubled. Local assembly facilities for both trucks and buses established in 1967 at Tabriz kicked off in the first year with a total of 2,962 units, a figure which increased to 5,597 in 1969. Local content steadily increased, leading to the formation in 1969 of the Iranian Diesel Engine Manufacturing Company. This was formed with local partners, Daimler-Benz owning 30 per cent. The company started supplying diesel engines for the locally-built Mercedes vehicles in 1970, but market conditions meant the number produced and assembled was small; 3,700 engines, for example, in 1971. This went up to 4,707 in 1972, but the profit situation was reported as not satisfactory. Nevertheless, Daimler-Benz ploughed more money into the facility, which led to a big increase in production to 10,961 engines in 1973.

This action undoubtedly benefitted the commercial vehicle operation, for in the same year Mercedes penetration of the Iranian truck market had reached 60 per cent and buses 90 per cent. From then on the expansion of this Iranian operation continued until the revolution in 1979, after which time the market plummeted, engine production dropping from well over 20,000 a year to less than 7,000, and operations were temporarily closed down.

Of course, there had been direct exports to many other countries in the Middle East for many years. However, following its success in Iran, Daimler-Benz turned its attention to Saudi Arabia, where commercial vehicle exports more than doubled to 4,000 units in 1974 and a partnership with the Mercedes-Benz distributor Jaffali & Bros was entered into at the beginning of 1975. The National Automobile Industry Company Ltd, of Jeddah, was founded as a result, with Daimler-Benz holding 26 per cent. In 1975, 7,600 vehicles, mainly heavy-duty models, were delivered to Saudi Arabia, a total which rose to 12,500 in 1976 and strengthened the decision to start assembly there in 1977. In the first full year of this assembly operation, 3,204 heavy-duty units were built, a figure which rose to 4,785 in the following year, with no less than 11 models in the truck programme.

Nigeria was one of the first African markets for direct exports from Germany in the 1950s, when this photograph was taken.

The moves to establish manufacturing or assembly facilities in overseas countries did not happen by accident. Many countries were trying to establish their own automotive industries. It was, accordingly, a deliberate policy of D-B to participate in their development with local partners where necessary. D-B stressed in its 1969 report the care with which it selected these projects. There were two basic requirements — adequate market potential and the existence of a

The advanced techniques employed at the Daimler-Benz overseas plants are reflected in this photograph of the advanced electro-phoretic paint shop at the Sao Paulo factory of Mercedes-Benz do Brasil.

favourable position regarding the supply industries. 'Without these basic requirements, the restrictive regulations and the consequent seclusion from world markets (*ie* the exclusion of free competition) usually give rise to additional costs with which the economy burdens itself.'

'The organization and corporate form of our assembly and manufacturing facilities is adapted to local conditions and regulations which differ from country to country. In appropriate circumstances these companies also take over sales and service operations.'

South Africa was another area which was due to see a formidable expansion by Daimler-Benz, but again it did not happen overnight. D-B obtained a 26.7 per cent stake in United Car and Diesel Distributors (Pty) Ltd, of Pretoria, in the 1960s. This company, through a wholly-owned subsidiary, was already the Mercedes-Benz importer for that country with sales then of 4,810 vehicles (cars and trucks).

Prospects, however, were uncertain for the South African company as the 1970s approached. Legislation about local manufacturing content made the company apprehensive about the future — with a situation envisaged by Daimler-Benz as being likely to raise production costs. The company commented at the time: 'The extent and profitability of future investments in South Africa will be influenced by the further development of this new situation.'

These apparent fears about the future appear to have been unfounded for, in the early-1970s, D-B's South African company moved steadily forward, mainly in cars rather than commercial vehicles, where sales stayed at around the 3,000 a year level in the first years of the decade, albeit in a relatively small market. The company's strength there was, however, in heavies rather than light commercial vehicles.

There was a boom in the South African economy in the mid-1970s and D-B's South African company benefitted, pushing up sales to 5,921 commercial vehicles in 1974 and 6,669 in 1975 before recession cut them back to 4,392 units in 1976 and 2,832 in 1977.

It was in 1978 that the most significant move for Daimler-Benz took place in this area of the world. Here's how it was reported by the company: 'To assure future sales of commercial vehicles in South Africa, Daimler-Benz made a bid to have Mercedes-Benz diesel engines manufactured under licence, in line with the South African industrialization policy. Against strong competition, licensing contracts for the manufacture of diesel engines were concluded at the end of 1978 by Perkins and Daimler-Benz with a company formed under the direction of the Government Industrial Development Corporation. The new plant will be built with exclusively South African capital in Atlantis, Cape Province, and will come on stream in 1981. The engines built in the plant will be used in the future by all motor vehicle manufacturers in South Africa.'

This subsequently was put into operation, with the Atlantis-project Daimler-Benz 400 series diesels being produced for installation in virtually every competitive make of truck on the South African market. The range made there covers nine engines including straight-five and six-cylinder units, V-8s, a V-10 and V-12s.

D-B's management had kept a close watch on markets in other parts of Africa. As a result, Daimler-Benz negotiated an agreement in 1975 with the Nigerian Government and, in the spring of 1977, the Anambra Motor Manufacturing Company Ltd was founded in the Enugu/Anambra State of Nigeria with a view to erecting a commercial vehicle plant. An assembly volume of 7,500 vehicles annually was planned by this company in which Daimler-Benz secured a 40 per cent interest, the remainder being owned by Nigerian Government and private interests. Initially, this was to be an assembly operation, with the components and parts required for assembly being delivered chiefly by the German domestic plants.

In Zambia, meanwhile, Kasama Vehicle Assemblers Ltd was founded in Lusaka in 1976 to build commercial vehicles. This was somewhat different from other overseas developments in that D-B secured a 15 per cent interest with Toyota also holding 15 per cent and the German Association for Economic Co-operation 10 per cent. The remaining shares were held by the Zambian State Development Company, INDECO.

In the 1970s, as well as its African ventures, Daimler-Benz turned its eyes on the Far East. In Indonesia, a 51 per cent

A robust specification is put to the test in the sugar cane plantations of Brazil. The L 2212 vehicle shown above is built for a gross combination weight of 32 tonnes. The lower picture is of a bonneted L 1421 tractor unit being operated in difficult conditions of heat and humidity, mud and poor road surfaces in Nigeria on timber haulage.

interest was gained in the import and distributing company PT Star Motors, of Jakarta. In a second deal, D-B joined with VW to acquire equal shares in PT German Motor Manufacturing, also of Jakarta, with a view to building Mercedes-Benz commercial vehicles and VW light transporters, starting in 1971. This venture got off to a good start with 1,000 Mercedes vehicles assembled and sold in the first year.

A move into Singapore followed the Indonesian venture, D-B taking 26 per cent of the stock in a new company, Supreme Star Engineering Pty Ltd, with a view to assembling 0306 model buses.

Predictably, with this ever-increasing spread of overseas interests, it was not always plain sailing in every territory. But the good outweighed the bad. The potential of the Australian truck market was always realized by Daimler-Benz. In fact D-B's Australian company was set up in the 1950s for both cars and goods vehicles. For many years, the numbers of commercial vehicles assembled there, however, was relatively small. Almost from the start, operations in Australia were

Bonneted cabs like this L 1824 unit are favoured in Saudi Arabia. This photograph shows the assembly operation in Jeddah.

Saudi Arabia is an important Middle-East market for Daimler-Benz. This is another view of the vehicle assembly line at Jeddah.

Extensive technical training programmes are run by Daimler-Benz for employees of its overseas plants. The group shown here were photographed in Lagos, Nigeria.

dogged by a mixture of unfavourable exchange rates, inflation and other external influences. Rarely in the 1970s, in fact, did sales exceed 1,000 commercial vehicles annually — and there were many buses in these figures. It was not until early in 1978 that Mercedes-Benz (Australia) Pty Ltd opened a heavy truck plant at Mulgrave, in Melbourne, and a much stronger hold obtained on the market.

There was also expansion in countries where Daimler-Benz had only distribution subsidiaries. This was concentrated in the late-1960s and 1970s on Europe, particularly the Common Market territories. For years in some countries outside Europe, like Australia, Daimler-Benz had its own sales and service companies, but this was not so in most of the others.

The 1970s saw this policy changed completely to the establishment of totally controlled subsidiaries. This enabled D-B to invest directly in sales and service facilities in each country so that dealers in effect had an extension of the D-B factory in their own country.

It was in France, in 1969, that D-B first started to pursue this policy, followed by Britain, in 1974, and in Belgium, Holland, Austria and Switzerland, in 1979. This obviously was a successful policy for an upturn in business occurred subsequently in every country concerned.

France was the test country for this policy. The Mercedes importer in France, Societe Financere des Etablissement Ch Delecroix SA, had, as indicated, become a majority-owned subsidiary and was renamed Mercedes-Benz France SA in 1969. Sales of commercial vehicles in 1968 had been 6,909 and the new company immediately built up from this.

Penetration of the French market hit a peak in 1973, with sales of 13,672 commercial vehicles. It dipped sharply to less than 10,000 in the market recession in France in 1975 before bouncing back even more strongly to 14,638 in 1976. This, however, was the peak year and sales have since steadied at between 12,000 and 13,000, with the exception of 1979, when they approached the 1976 record.

In Italy, the new company formed was called Mercedes-Benz Italia SpA. It was formed in 1973 with Daimler-Benz taking a 75 per cent holding, with the remainder being taken by D-B's Italian representative, Autostar SpA. It was announced that a stronger market penetration in the Italian commercial vehicle market was being sought. There was no immediate success, however, for the oil crisis of 1973 had particularly severe affects on the market and the general economy in Italy, where the exchange rate deteriorated steadily. Nevertheless, after a poor first year, when the company sold 603 vehicles, sales were pushed up to 1,844 in the second year and to 2,342 in 1975, despite the market there sinking by 25 per cent overall. D-B, however, consolidated on the Italian market in the following year, with sales leaping by 75 per cent. The peak there was hit in 1979, with sales of 5,175 commercial vehicles.

Relatively, Mercedes-Benz success in the UK had been modest in the 1950s and 1960s, but Britain's entry of the European Economic Community marked a big change for the UK's commercial vehicle industry. The establishment in 1974 of a new subsidiary in Britain, Mercedes Benz (United

The L 608 shown here picking up coffee beans is one of the lighter classes of vehicle built at Daimler-Benz's Brazilian factory.

Kingdom) Ltd, was a significant step for Daimler-Benz. In spite of a depressed economy in Britain at this time, sales moved up immediately from 1,407 in 1973 to 2,322. After a small drop in the following year, the company steadily increased sales to close on 7,000 in 1979 before being hit by the depression.

D-B experienced a similar steady increase in sales in the 1970s in both Holland and Belgium, sales rising to close to 11,000 commercial vehicles in 1979 in Holland and just over 4,000 in Belgium before the general recession led to a drop in sales in both countries in 1980.

Outside the Common Market, D-B's interests centred on Spain, Yugoslavia, Austria and Switzerland. In Spain, a new company was formed in the February of 1969 called Compania Hispano Alemana de Productos Mercedes-Benz, in which Daimler-Benz held a 50.5 per cent share.

The aim of this was to bring together the company's sales and manufacturing operations in Spain, including the car and commercial vehicle plant in Barcelona. An indication of the reason for this development is given in the 1969 D-B company report which says: 'The efforts by Spain to join the Common Market increase the chances of that country becoming a more accessible market in the future.'

In 1972, this Spanish company was merged with the VW subsidiary, IMOSA, to form a new company called Compania Hispano Alemana de Productos Mercedes-Benz y Volkswagen SA (MEVOSA for short). D-B and VW each had a 26.8 per cent holding in this, with the Spanish Government state-owned concern INI holding 25 per cent and minority shareholders the rest. Although D-B reported that production of the OM 636 engine and manufacture of the Mercedes-Benz light van and bus range and a derivative of the VW light van range had been stepped up, the earnings situation was still unsatisfactory, largely due to strikes and the poor state of the Spanish economy.

This continued to be the general situation throughout the 1970s. A bright spot, against the trend, was the success of the improved version of the B 1000 purpose-built light van in 1975. In spite of this, losses continued and in 1976 output was down 25 per cent, primarily through strikes and changes in currency exchange rates and devaluation.

It was in this year that D-B took over ownership of VW's shareholding, but a change in the share structure gave D-B a 42.7 per cent holding, with INI holding the rest. The situation improved towards the end of the 1970s, a period during which D-B stepped up investment as Spain's entry of the Common Market was thought to be approaching.

Daimler-Benz consolidated on the Spanish market in 1981 when a new company in Spain was set up called Mercedes-Benz Espana SA. This followed the acquisition of 52.7 per cent of the shares of MEVOSA.

Negotiations to obtain a majority interest in MEVOSA began in 1980 when the German company reached agreement with INI to increase MEVOSA's capital by 420 million pesetas, all underwritten by Daimler-Benz. These increases in capital formed part of a major 5,000 million peseta investment plan, which involved modernization and an increase in capacity at the Vitoria and Barcelona works.

Daimler-Benz's moves in Jugoslavia occurred in the early-1970s. A major investment and development programme was started in 1973 in co-operation with FAP-FAMOS, of Belgrade, with the aim of producing 10,000 vehicles a year, one half of them models in the existing vehicle production programme and the rest — in due course — Mercedes. These were initially middleweight vehicles, (1213s) although 14-tonners and heavier models were introduced later.

The number of Mercedes models remained relatively small at first, but rose steadily to 1,727 in 1979 out of the 6,829 commercial vehicles produced. An increase in the number of Mercedes vehicles was anticipated as production of additional models was planned.

Traditionally, Daimler-Benz had connections with Austria and these came to the fore at the end of the 1970s with the German company combining with Steyr-Daimler-Puch in a company called Gelaendefahrzeug Gesellschaft, based in Graz, to produce cross-country vehicles. Each had a 50 per cent interest and, of the 2,800 vehicles built in the first year, 2,500 carried the Mercedes name badge. D-B, however, relinquished its financial interest in this development in 1981.

As part of D-B's programme of obtaining a more direct control over its European sales distribution activities, a 50 per cent interest in Daimler-Benz Oesterreich Vertriebsgesellschaft mbH, with a head office in Salzburg, was obtained on January 1, 1980. A total of 4,644 Mercedes commercial vehicles were sold in Austria in 1979 and D-B announced its intention to strengthen its position on the Austrian market.

In the early-1970s, Daimler-Benz sold strongly in the relatively small Swiss market. The company had a controlling interest in one of its distributors, Handelsgesellschaft Fuer Daimler-Benz Erzeugnisse AG, of Zurich, through which it sold some 2,000 vehicles in the peak year of 1973. A 50 per cent interest in another distribution company, Merfag AG, of Zurich, was purchased in the following year.

This company sold 1,440 Mercedes commercial vehicles in 1974, compared with 1,997 in 1973 and adding to 1,363 of the older-established distributor. These figures indicated a big slide in sales in Switzerland with sales in 1975 at the older distributor falling to 646 and at the new one to 885.

Things then steadily improved with sales in 1979 hitting an all-time high. Merfag became general distributor of Mercedes cars on January 1, 1980, D-B having increased its shareholding to 51 per cent and the company's name to

The need to tailor models to the requirements of overseas markets is reflected in this Mercedes-Benz 2632 for Switzerland, where gross weights are much lower than in other European countries, but the power-to-weight ratio required is the highest. Thus a 320-bhp engine is fitted in this Swiss-registered six-wheeler to operate at 25 tonnes gross weight.

Mercedes Benz (Schwiez) AG.

In 1980, D-B also obtained a minority interest in FBW, a small Swiss truck manufacturer. Amongst other things it gave D-B the opportunity to build narrow-cab vehicles of a type required under Swiss law and other 'specials'.

Of all the markets in the world to which vehicle manufacturers look for business, the USA stands out as the prime example, and Daimler-Benz was no exception in this respect. D-B, having established itself securely there with private cars in the 1950s and 1960s, felt it was only a question of waiting for the right opportunity to break into the commercial vehicle world. This did not occur until the 1970s, and by then D-B was ready.

The company had started exporting commercial vehicles to the USA from Germany in 1970, but the then high value of the dollar and other controls militated against success. It was, in fact, from the development of the Brazilian company that the first quantity supply of commercial vehicles was made to the USA. In 1975, these totalled 1,200 vehicles. An importing centre, with sales office, inspection facilities, spare parts centre and workshop facilities, was established at Jacksonville, Florida. Sales steadily increased, from 1,243 in 1976, to 1,863 in 1977 and to 2,607 in 1978.

By this time, Daimler-Benz was planning an assembly operation and, in the meantime, the existing sales area and dealer network were enlarged. Numbers of vehicles sold in the USA reached 3,950 units in 1979 and Daimler-Benz saw the main scope for expansion in the 9-tonnes to 15-tonnes gvw truck class, where there was a steady trend towards fitment of diesel engines, rather than the traditional US practice of fitting petrol-powered units.

The plans for an assembly operation forged ahead and in 1980 work started on the construction of the assembly plant sited at Hampton, Virginia. The initial planned capacity of this was 6,000 medium-duty trucks, made from components supplied from the company's Brazilian and German plants.

The assembly plant at Hampton represented an investment in building and land of 8.1 million dollars. The first model the plant started producing was the L 1116 truck, with a gross weight of 25,000 lb and powered by the 160-bhp turbocharged diesel engine. Subsequently, the company started to assemble its second model, the L 1316 (30,000 gvw) at Hampton, followed by the LS 1418 city tractor.

Then, early in 1981, came the announcement that Daimler-Benz and Consolidated Freightways Inc, of San Francisco, had signed a letter of intent for the sale of Consolidated's subsidiary, Freightliner, the US heavy-vehicle manufacturer, to Daimler-Benz for 225 million dollars. Freightliner builds heavy vehicles in the US class 8, from 15 tonnes upwards, in the USA and Canada.

Freightliner has its headquarters and main factory in Portland, Oregon, and factories in Indianapolis, Indiana, Mt Holly, North Carolina, and Burnaby, in Canada. In 1980, the company built 11,000 trucks of over 15 tonnes gross weight, accounting for 9 per cent of the US market in this sector. Although obviously there is much still to be done, D-B must have an exciting future in the USA as a result of this move.

As the 1970s began, Daimler-Benz was already a world force in truck manufacture. By the end of the decade it had become Europe's most successful truck producer on the world scene. What was the reason for this? There is no doubt that a main cause was the enlightened policy adopted with regard to the overseas manufacturing and assembling companies. Profits earned by them were not creamed off, but left with them for financing further expansion. Added to this, in order to make use of the international money market for financing future activities, finance companies were set up in 1970 in Zurich and Luxembourg to provide the money so essential for the success of the overseas ventures undertaken by Daimler-Benz.

Chapter 7

The future: Energy and the environment

As Daimler-Benz moves strongly ahead in the 1980s, it is perhaps the most impressive commercial vehicle manufacturer in the world. Pundits in the industry are constantly predicting that the number of commercial vehicle makers will dwindle to four or five by the year 2000. If this happens — and I am not convinced that it will — Daimler-Benz would get my vote as the company most likely to survive. The work conducted, however, has not been confined to the distant future; much of it has had an immediate significance.

The 1970s was a particularly fruitful period in this respect, for it saw Daimler-Benz introduce a wide variety of services to operators, ranging from systems to aid cost control to those designed to simplify vehicle selection and purchases. Product development also reflected the fact that the company thought very deeply about its customers and their problems.

When the New Generation cab range was evolved, great pains were taken to make it look less aggressive than many comparable heavy goods vehicles, the public's animosity to goods vehicles everywhere having grown in parallel with the increase in international haulage. A survey conducted amongst housewives in England in 1975 found the Mercedes-Benz 1626S to have the lowest 'aggressive' rating of seven vehicles presented to them in driving tests, with the Mercedes LPS 1418 having the second least aggressive rating. This is just one example of many efforts made by Daimler-Benz to make heavy vehicles more acceptable environmentally. Both noise and exhaust emissions have also been constantly studied with a view to improving engine characteristics in both of these areas.

Daimler-Benz, of course, has also been researching alternative fuels for road vehicle propulsion with a view to reducing pollution. One of the most promising projects has been the use of hydrogen in a converted petrol engine, and in 1979 the company followed up its original van application of such a system (in 1977) with a small city bus based on the Bremen van chassis.

Apart from being an apparently viable alternative to petrol, hydrogen has the advantage of producing a very clean exhaust, making it particularly suitable for use in urban areas. Among the necessary modifications to the petrol engine was the fitting of a high-performance ignition system (as is recommended for LPG burning) and a water-injection unit.

In such a design the hydrogen is stored in metal-hydride tanks, from which it is released by the application of heat. This heat can come from the coolant, the exhaust, or the warm air in the passenger compartment. A disadvantage of hydrogen propulsion is weight, a 200-kg hydride tank providing the energy equivalent of only about 16 kg of petrol.

D-B's investigations have been extended to embrace the utilization of the engine's waste heat for other purposes, thus ensuring the minimum consumption of the world's precious energy resources. D-B has also investigated a hybrid system in

Daimler-Benz has been acutely aware of the need to make trucks look less 'aggressive' in their styling. Here, housewives are being invited to give ratings to vehicles to reveal how environmentally intrusive were a number of different makes of truck. This is the Mercedes-Benz entry, an LPS 1418, being demonstrated with badges obscured.

which hydrogen is mixed with pure benzine before being fed to the engine.

Alternative vehicle fuels of vegetable origin, and therefore virtually inexhaustible, have also been extensively probed into by D-B, mainly in Brazil. Ethanol (ethyl alcohol) has long been known as a valid petrol substitute or additive, and Daimler-Benz's Brazilian affiliate, Mercedes-Benz do Brasil, has been heavily involved in researching alternative diesel fuels. It proved at a top-level demonstration in 1979 that a Mercedes bus could operate on vegetable-derived fuel without requiring any major modification to the engine. The bus was actually run first on diesel fuel and then, unchanged, on a mixture of ethanol and an ignition accelerator; the only preparation for dual-fuel operation was some minor tuning of the injection pump.

Methanol and ethanol, when pure, are unsuitable for the conventional diesel engine. However, the fact that methanol evaporates at a temperature as low as 65 degrees C (149 degrees F) gave Daimler-Benz engineers the idea of burning the evaporated fuel (gas) in a gas engine, the energy required for evaporation being derived from the engine heat. This normally is dissipated via the radiator and the exhaust system to the environment. With gas even more energy is saved, D-B points out, because the fan consumes less power than that of a diesel engine.

As a result, an alcohol-gas engine was developed based on the M 407 hG, a gas engine developed by Daimler-Benz some time earlier from a six-cylinder diesel engine. This was originally designed for the use of natural gas and propane or butane. Several components from the original diesel engine,

In recent years there has been extensive research at Daimler-Benz into the aerodynamic characteristics of commercial vehicles. This has resulted in a range of spoilers tailored to the needs of Mercedes-Benz vehicles.

for example, the pistons, cylinder-heads, valves and exhaust manifold, as well as the combustion chambers, were designed to burn gaseous fuels on the spark-ignition principle with the ignition unit also adapted to allow combustion of gaseous

The use of hydrogen as a fuel is one of the areas of experiment to find an alternative fuel to petrol and diesel. Both small buses and goods vehicles fuelled by hydrogen have been put into experimental service. Here is a small bus based on the Bremen light transporter chassis powered by hydrogen and developing a 50-kW power output.

methanol.

Mention should also be made of Daimler-Benz's work on automotive gas turbine engine development. This, in Daimler-Benz's view, however, is not a viable proposition for road vehicles. The gas turbine is still, Daimler-Benz considers, uneconomic with relatively high production costs. It is a very reliable and long-lasting power unit, however, and ceramics development could, it is considered, mean an improvement in fuel efficiency.

Then there have been experiments with electric power. At the beginning of 1979, 20 OE 305 hybrid electric buses went into service in Stuttgart and elsewhere, with the blessing of the West German Federal Ministry for research. These buses, which look entirely conventional, are battery-powered in central urban areas where pollution problems are greatest. In suburban and out-of-town districts they switch to their diesel

Extensive work on the development of engines using alternative fuels to petroleum-based products has been conducted by Daimler-Benz. Much of this research and development has been conducted in Brazil with vegetable oils. Methanol-powered engines and hybrid methanol-diesel engines have resulted. Here, an experimental bus using an alternative fuel is being demonstrated.

One of four ethanol-powered buses in regular service in the city of Sao Paulo, in Brazil. Only minor adjustments to a traditional diesel engine's injection system are necessary.

as the primary energy source.

The diesels drive generators to supply current for propelling the buses and for recharging the batteries. Consequently they run at constant speed in the optimum regime for low pollutants and low consumption. Since they have acoustic insulation, their noise level is also low — another environmental advantage.

Incidentally, Mercedes Duo buses were operating in Esslingen from 1975. These vehicles were hybrid trolleybuses since they took their power from overhead wires in central urban areas, beyond which the trolley arm was retracted and battery or diesel propulsion was used.

Another electric vehicle project of D-B's was the LF 306 battery-powered van, quite a number of which were put into service for delivery duties in West German cities. This vehicle had a payload of 1.5 tonnes and its operating radius was stated to be about 65 km. The vehicle was so designed that when the batteries ran down they could either be recharged

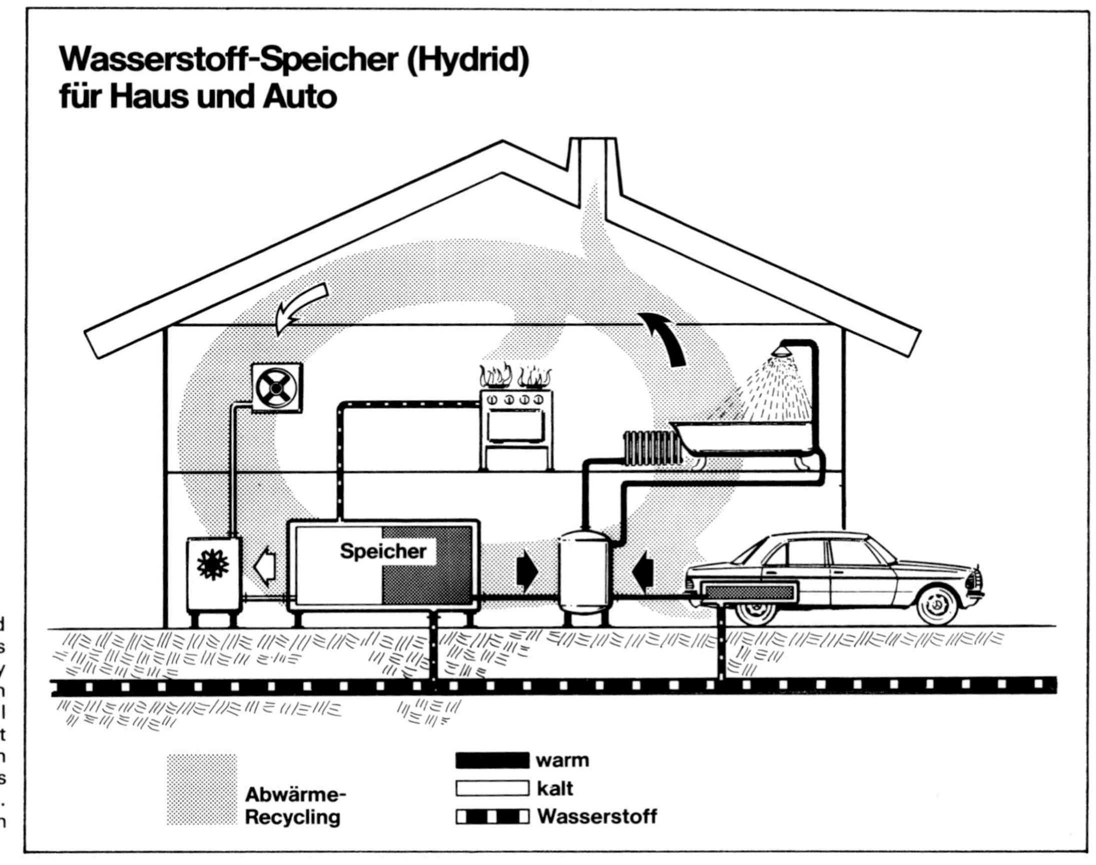

As a spin-off from its hydrogen-powered vehicle developments, Daimler-Benz has widened its horizons and the company points out that the fact that hydrogen can be chemically absorbed by metal hydrides, and can thus be stored without any risk, opens up wide application possibilities as this plan of a house and its possible heating arrangement shows. Note, too, that vehicles can be run from the same fuel source.

In the goods vehicle safety sector one of the most notable developments is that of the Mercedes-Benz/Wabco ABS anti-lock braking system. In truck/trailer combinations, fitment of ABS prevents breakaway of the trailer and an articulated vehicle from jack-knifing on heavy braking. In demonstrations, the better braking of ABS (top) is shown by the markings on the wheels.

from the mains or replaced by a fully charged pack — a changeover that took only a few minutes. An improved version of the electro-van was subsequently based on the Bremen chassis.

There were also investigations into engine/flywheel energy systems using regenerative braking to 'recharge' the flywheel. The D-B system propels the vehicle purely by flywheel energy. Fitted on urban buses, the flywheel is used in conjunction with a diesel engine — which also recharges the flywheel — in other circumstances.

Apart from seeking alternative fuels to diesel, D-B has also been involved in many other aspects of energy-saving, not least the significance of aerodynamics and their influence on fuel consumption. A full research programme was undertaken in the late-1970s into the conditions under which an air deflector should be used. Using cabs with low air-resistance characteristics and selecting the most suitable major components results in a notable saving in fuel at higher speeds, D-B found. Accordingly, an air deflector was developed by Daimler-Benz for mounting on all New Generation cabs to give maximum fuel economy for vehicles with high bodies.

Extensive work has been done by D-B to improve commercial vehicle safety levels. The company's programme has been a wide one, but nowhere has it been more successful than in braking, notably in the development of ABS anti-lock braking, made available as a standard option early in 1981 on heavy-duty trucks and buses for the German market and later in other countries.

Four single-chip micro-computers are used in the ABS anti-lock braking system. The system, developed in parallel with that fitted on Mercedes private cars, was originally announced for trucks and buses at the 1979 Frankfurt Motor Show. It departed from the principle used in the anti-locking systems in that the latter devices employ an electronic sensing device, which senses the speed of the wheel or axle and, when locking is imminent, a solenoid valve operates to reduce brake-cylinder pressure to prevent the wheel from locking.

The ABS system takes things a stage further. A toothed wheel and sensor are fitted on each wheel to detect the rotation speed. This feeds a 16-bit micro-computer, which analyzes the signals and sends messages to a solenoid valve, which operates in the same way as on other anti-lock equipment. The ABS system was developed jointly between Daimler-Benz and the Hanover, West Germany-based company of Westinghouse Air Brake Company (WABCO).

From the outside of the vehicle, fitment of the system was recognizable by two rectangular shapes at the front — the transmitting and receiving antennae for the radar equipment. This work is still going on. The driver sees a lighted strip of variable length above the speedometer. This strip changes in colour from green, to amber to denote caution, and red, these colours indicating whether there is sufficient distance between the vehicle and the obstruction in front of it. If the vehicle is too close, a warning signal is also heard. As the danger increases, the short warning pips become one continuous sound.

The equipment must be pre-programmed by the driver, since a wet or slippery road affects the rate of deceleration when braking and so alters the safe following distance. The driver must allow for this by pressing one of three keys for dry, wet or icy road conditions.

The emphasis of Daimler-Benz's engineering work for immediate application in the late-1970s and 1980 was on the improvement of specific fuel consumption values and on the better adaption of engine, transmission and axle ratio to the different vehicle models and operating conditions. The company's engine range was enlarged by turbocharged, charge air-cooled V-8 engines with favourable torque.

These V-8 power units formed parts of what Daimler-Benz from 1979 onwards called its 420 series (previously the 400 series) engines. They were the outcome of this philosophy of high performance (particularly high torque) and low fuel consumption. The company is proud of achieving extremely low specific fuel consumption figures for this range — the equivalent of an excellent 43 per cent engine efficiency level. It is also regarded as of particular merit bearing in mind that

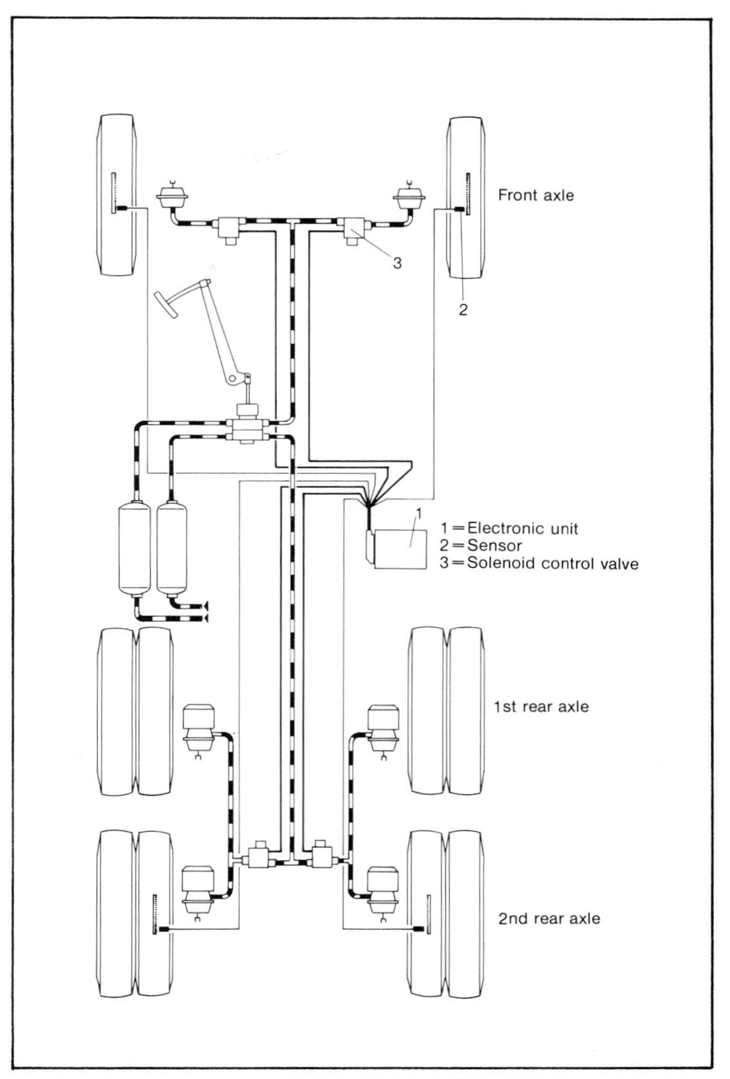

A typical layout of the Mercedes-Benz/Wabco ABS anti-lock braking system on a 6 × 4 tractor unit for articulated vehicle operation.

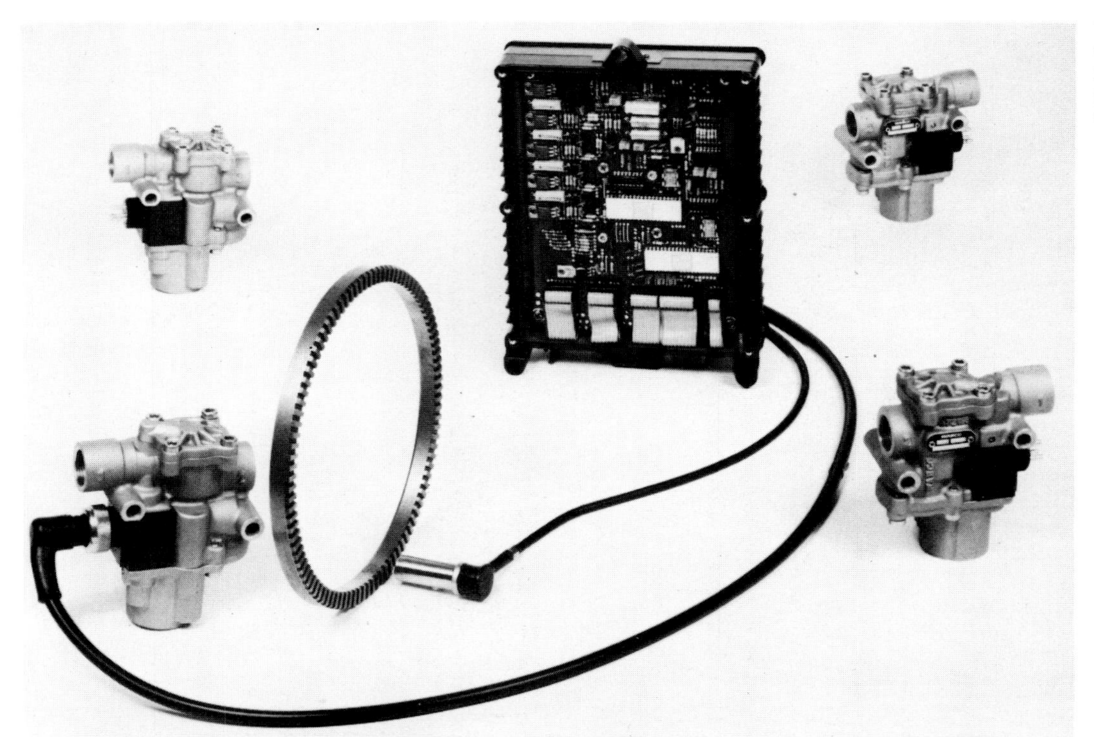

The ABS components for commercial vehicles are the microcomputer control unit, toothed wheels and sensors for all four wheels, and four solenoid control valves.

30 per cent of total diesel-powered vehicle costs are represented by fuel.

The engine philosophy at D-B can be seen as part of a broader attitude which says, 'we are not just a manufacturer limited only to the development, production and sale of trucks, but we have a total involvement in road transport'. Consequently, Daimler-Benz has a remarkably extensive commitment to research and development into road transport as a whole. To this end, the characteristics of every component, quite apart from each vehicle model, are looked at from every kind of angle to make sure they achieve the optimum, commercially, environmentally and functionally.

Whilst a basic aim is to produce a vehicle which secures maximum operating profit for the user, it is essential, says D-B, also to ensure that the design is such that the driver is able to carry out his job in the best manner possible and with the least possible strain. This is a very important part of the company's attitude to road safety. In this context, making sure that the specification of a vehicle makes it compatible with other traffic on the road is given equal importance.

Daimler-Benz lays stress on developing vehicles specifically to suit the market, the individual customer and the job the vehicle has to do. Just how far the company is prepared to go to make this philosophy work is reflected in the computer software packages developed as a customer service. These range from computer-assisted vehicle selection to route planning. Two particularly useful ones for the fleet-user are TRASCO and OPEZ. TRASCO is a traffic-simulation

One of the main experiments into alternative power being conducted by Daimler-Benz is with hybrid electrobuses. Twenty of these are in experimental operation (to 1985) in Germany. In inner city areas, the buses rely on electric power from batteries. In outer areas, they switch to the conventional diesel engines with which the vehicles are also fitted.

Methanol derived from coal is being used experimentally in a number of Mercedes-Benz buses operating in Germany.

programme which helps the fleet owner to select the optimum drive train. OPEZ determines the optimum point or date for replacement of vehicles.

Other useful schemes for the user include the company's Fleet Information System, which contributes to cost control and maximum fleet performance by monitoring, controlling and forecasting operators' long and short-term running costs. There are other schemes as well, like those providing maintenance and repair contracts and quality assurance on the purchase of secondhand Mercedes vehicles.

These are, however, just a few relevant examples of the many thought-provoking programmes of D-B into commercial vehicles of the immediate and distant future. They are part of the Group's on-going plans to improve trucks and make them more acceptable environmentally. They reflected, too, the fact that Daimler-Benz ended the 1970s even more strongly than it began them. What, then, was the situation statistically for D-B as the 1980s dawned and what were the prospects?

Daimler-Benz feels that the future technology of the truck will be determined by the need for even more economy. The trucks of the 1980s will have more powerful engines, but will be more economical as a result of optimized drive trains and the application of electronic devices. The company sees greater use of aluminium and synthetic materials in chassis and truck components to reduce weight. It also sees greater standardization of regulations between countries governing vehicle construction directly influencing design of vehicles and components.

D-B reported in 1981 that in spite of the fact that its plants were operating at full capacity, it was not able to meet all demands in 1980. Worldwide output climbed 6.4 per cent to 272,868 commercial vehicles. Daimler-Benz's domestic plants produced more than 200,000 units for the first time (+7.6 per cent) and its South American subsidiaries 69,827 units (+3.1 per cent). (A strike in the company's Brazilian factory prevented stronger expansion in South America.)

At 85,845 units, new registrations of Mercedes commercial vehicles in the Federal Republic of Germany almost equalled the high level of the preveious year (87,846) and an increase of 2 per cent to 26,000 units was obtained in the van market (up to 4 tonnes gvw).

The company raised truck exports of its whole range by 21.9 per cent to 105,526 units. Demand from OPEC countries and several African states was especially strong. In Western Europe the company was also able to increase sales substantially in several important markets, notably Italy and Switzerland. These figures show that there is no slackening, at present, in the momentum of D-B's progress, and there is no sign of this happening in spite of the world truck depression. The company's US venture must be the key to further expansion, with the potential there still to be fulfilled.